Copyright © 2024
by Sarah Bamford Seidelmann

ISBN: 978-0-9860692-9-1

All rights Reserved.
No part of this book may be reproduced or used in any manner without written permission of the copyright owner except for the use of quotations in a book review.

For more information contact
sarah@followyourfeelgood.com

Find the author at followyourfeelgood.com

 **FIRST EDITION**

Cover and interior art by Sarah Bamford Seidelmann

Cover and interior graphic design by Drai of
Wild Redhead Design, goddessdrai@gmail.com

Edited by Grace Kerina, gracekerina.com

All illustrations are the creations of the author and illustrator with the exception of those that are in the public domain.

# BOUNDARIES MAKE LOVE POSSIBLE

### Self-Respecting Boundaries
#### Illustrated

#### BOOK 7 OF THE
Sarah Bamford Seidelmann
#### Collection

> ***Swimming with Elephants*** is an entertaining and moving front row seat in the drama that unfolds when a western-trained physician does the work required to become a true healer.
>
> —Christiane Northrup, MD, NY Times best-selling author of *Goddesses Never Age*
>
> ***The Book of Beasties*** guides readers into a profound understanding of the personal messages offered through spirit animals. Detailing the techniques for applying their transformative, healing medicine, Seidelmann empowers us to dissolve the boundaries between what is seen and interpreted by the outer physical eye and the inner eye of the soul.
>
> —Michael Bernard Beckwith, author of *Life Visioning*
>
> Seidelmann is an often irreverent narrator whose memoir is as transformative as it is off-the-wall. Told with a mix of humor, raw honesty, and gentleness, ***Swimming with Elephants*** is a journey of healing. Her willingness to be herself and to follow her path, no matter how non-traditional and wacky it might seem at first, makes for an endearing and illuminating adventure.
>
> —Foreward Reviews
>
> Seidelmann's transcribed instructions from Alice the Elephant in *How Good Are You Willing to Let It Get?* bring a sense of higher meaning, softness, humor, and beauty to our human voyage through a difficult world. Sarah is a true medicine woman, and everything she creates is good for what ails us."
>
> Martha Beck, author of *Expecting Adam* and *Finding Your Way in a Wild New World*
>
> Born to FREAK is hysterical and wise! I read it on the plane and people next to me must have thought I was crazy, I kept laughing so much. This is the perfect book for you if you love to laugh and have trouble fitting in."
>
> Amy Pearson, Master Coach and Instructor for Martha Beck Inc. and author of the forthcoming memoir, *Forgiving Amy*

For **Joel Thomas Mitchell Bamford, MD,** the GREATEST DAD in the whole world.

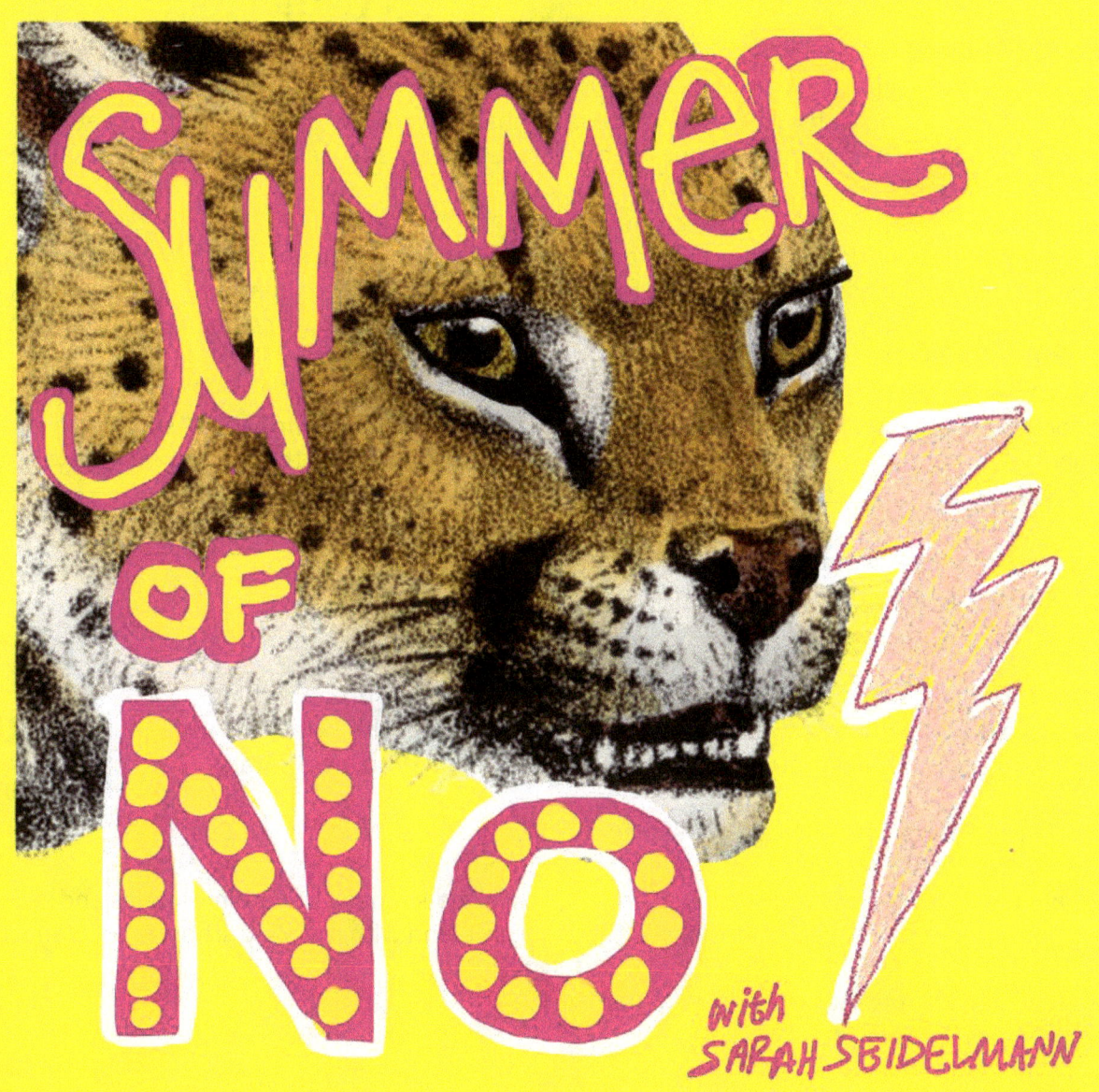

No. 6

# Wild and Free Again!

## introduction.

In the summer of 2021, along with 36 other brave souls, I embarked on a 100-day Creative Soul Retrieval, an experience where we intended to call back the part of our souls that loves to express itself—our inner artist, dancer, singer, poet, writer, painter, and/or musician.

The idea for my project to do for those hundred days came while cleaning my office, when I discovered an old handwritten list of boundaries that I had written for myself around my professional work. Just six months after writing it, I realized that *I had already broken most of the self-protective boundaries I had committed to.* That shocked me. *Why* hadn't I kept those boundaries?

My name for the project, "My Summer of No: 100 Days of Self-Respecting Boundaries," sounded breezy and freeing, not shockingly transformative, but like many creative projects, it took me to the places I wasn't even aware I needed to go. It's not hyperbole to say this project changed my life.

- I much more easily set boundaries at work.
- I have *much* more time to be creative.
- My marriage is in the process of being reborn.

And, just this morning, I responded (cheerfully) to an email request to do something I did not want to do, by writing back, "Thank you for thinking of me. This doesn't work for me. I look forward to seeing you next month at the gathering! With love, Sarah."

I barely recognized myself. No apology. No explanation. Clean. Clear. No guilt. Just *no*.

**CLEAN. CLEAR. JUST NO.**

The summer I did that Creative Soul Retrieval project, I received so many private messages and texts from friends describing boundary-related aha! realizations as they tagged along with my daily art posts and reflections.

Here are a few of those messages, shared with permission:

"

It's hardest for me to set boundaries with my 25yr old daughter. Mostly because I want to be there for her whenever she's in need. Because my mom was NOT there for me. I never want my daughter to feel like she's a bother.

I am learning from you that I get to express my emotions and be myself and that does not give someone the liberty to cross my boundary. I think I used to believe that I deserve my boundary to be crossed when I show love.

After leaving a somewhat co-dependent relationship with a man with many narcissistic traits, I find that I've really distanced myself from most of the people I can't easily say no to. I know this is not the same as setting healthy boundaries, but I'm just not there yet on my healing journey. I have put in the work to have healthy boundaries with my mom and am glad I did.

Work- I struggle saying no to work!

My daughter... she has intense insomnia cycles and wants me to stay up with her...when that happens it is so hard to say no to that. Even knowing how much lack of sleep derails me.

My son XXXX! He's very independent so when he asks for something ($40.00 for Chik Fil A $40.00!!!) I find myself saying yes, and I throw some gas $$ in as well.

I struggle to say no to my mom. I'm not sure I've ever said no to my mom. I love her. And I'm exhausted. I've trained her how to need me all the time.

I loved this project and followed it daily. I am turning into a boundary boss, now. I stopped going to meetings that didn't add value to my days, I am sitting in the unknown rather than settling for a known that isn't for me, I have created space from people who do not have my best interest in mind... I can create my own safe space rather than needing to armor up which [is what] I was doing when I didn't know how to keep myself safe before... a new skill for me!!!"

"

From all the messages I received, I realized that so many of my *favorite* people were, like me, desperately needing to shore up the fences around their personal time and space so they could ramble wild and free again.

I hope this book inspires you to create some beautiful boundaries for yourself and in your family! I've learned that boundaries *make love possible*.

With big love,
Sarah

SARAH

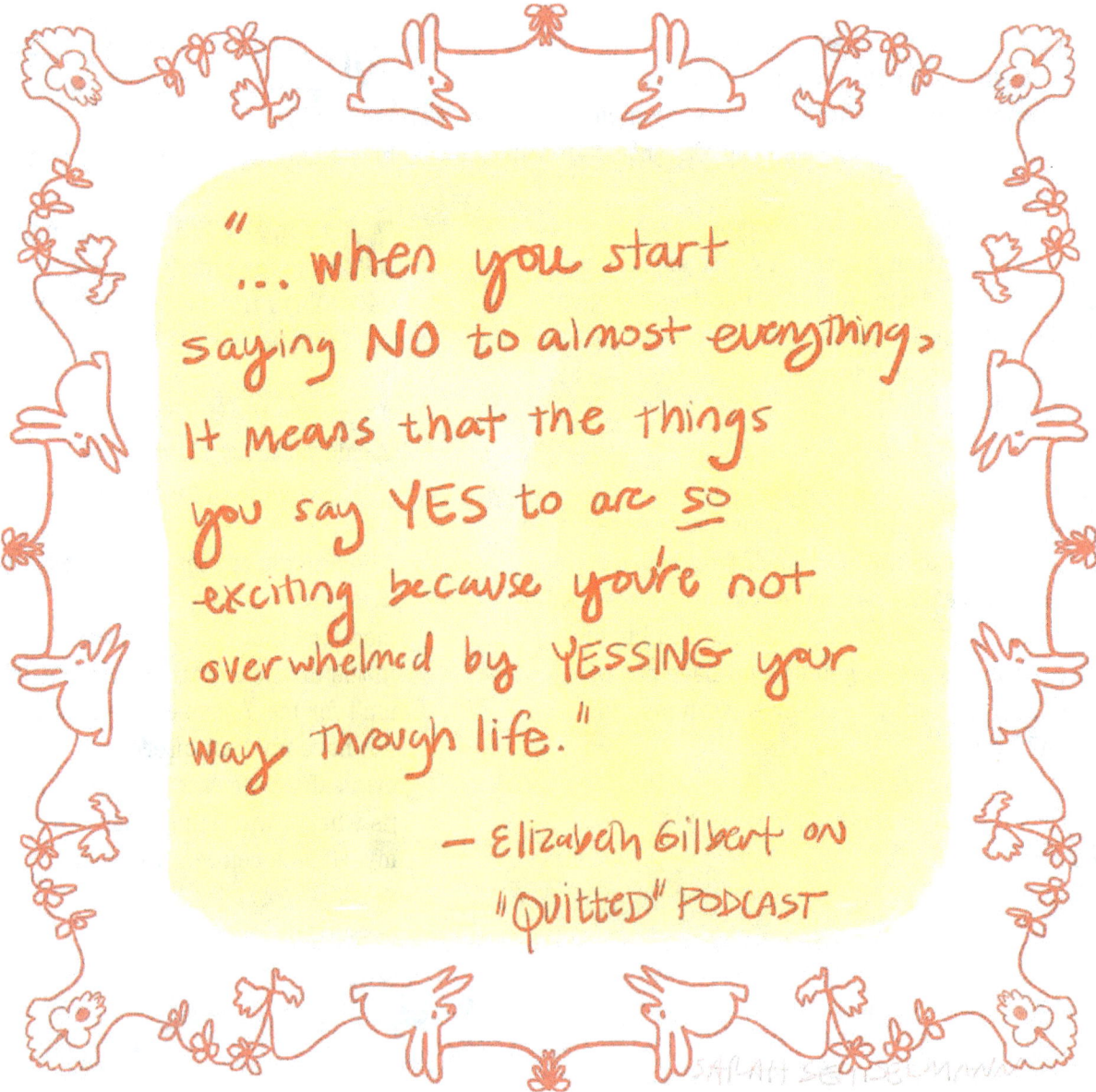

"...when you start saying NO to almost everything, It means that the things you say YES to are so exciting because you're not overwhelmed by YESSING your way through life."

— Elizabeth Gilbert on "QUITTED" PODCAST

# Compassionate People Say NO

## they say NO when they need to.

Lordy, I want to be loved and accepted. Heck, even celebrated, with a brass band and sexy fire dancers. So, a part of me fantasizes about, politely, saying no to some **perfectly reasonable requests**, such as:

Nice Person: "Can you please chair this committee? You've got so many good ideas!"

Me: "No."

OR

Super Nice Person: "Would you write a chapter in my book? It would mean the *world* to me!"

Me: "No."

In the past, I deeply believed that saying no to those people would mean that I was a horrible, ungrateful, selfish, and unloving sort of person.

My inner third-grader people-pleaser (she's sporting brown-suede earth shoes, a tiered chintz prairie skirt, glasses with '70s tinted lenses, and *a very solemn look on her face*) cringes at the idea of refusing people. She's worried that people will feel hurt or (gasp!) that *they* will believe that we (she and I!) are mean or insensitive or uncaring.

Recently, my brilliant friend and colleague, author Inger Kenobi, reminded me that Brené Brown says that *the opposite is true*:

"Compassionate people say no when they need to, and when they say yes, they mean it. They are compassionate because their boundaries keep them out of resentment." –Brene Brown

Brené says this is a *fact*: **The best, *kindest*, and most loving people say no when they need to.** Her actual smarty-pants-in-a-lab research supports it.

To be more compassionate, I must say no whenever necessary.

---

## Dear Magnificent Me,

**Can you remember a time** when you became resentful and behaved in a not at all compassionate way because you said yes to something you'd wanted to say no to?

**What boundary** would you set today to move towards becoming a more compassionate person?

## Dear Great Mystery,

Please help me to say no each and every time it is necessary, so that I can grow in compassion.

# Am I Saying YES To Avoid Feelings?
### feeeeeling feelings.

When we first muster the courage to set a healthy boundary, we discover that others do not always like it. Maybe the first boundary you set went swimmingly, but at some point it happened to you:

## Other people had BIG FEELINGS about the boundary you set.

One Christmas, our eleven-year-old daughter requested that only one of our several days of celebration be quiet and calm and with "just our family"—meaning no other relatives, friends, cousins, grandparents, etc. We felt that was a reasonable request and wanted to honor her desire for quiet and intimacy. When I let my beloved mother know that we planned to spend either Christmas Eve or Christmas Day with her and my dad, but not both days, she felt deeply hurt. The last thing I wanted to do was hurt her. I felt forced to choose between supporting my daughter or making my mom feel better. We held our daughter's boundary, got through it, and eventually my mom let it go and all was well.

So, there's a *very solid* reason I'm now scared to set a boundary. Somebody's feelings could get hurt.

I have avoided setting boundaries to protect myself from having to experience the strong feelings of others (disappointment, anger, shock, grief, surprise, sadness) many times. Especially with my parents, partner, and kids, but others too: fellow committee members, colleagues, and friends. Intellectually, I know that other people's emotional reactions belong to them but that doesn't seem to make it any easier.

So, I gently remind myself that I can set boundaries and allow people to have their feelings. I am not God, and I can't control the world. But I can tend to my beautiful little part of the world by taking responsibility for creating and protecting my space.

# Dear Magnificent Me,

**Whose BIG feelings** might you be trying to avoid right now by avoiding boundary-setting?

**What boundary would you set** if you knew that it would all (eventually) be OK?

# Dear Great Mystery,

Please give me the **PEACE** to weather the storm of other people's reactions as I set the boundaries that HELP ME (OR MY FAMILY) THRIVE.

# REMEMBER
## Don't Miss Out on What Matters Most...
### be responsible for yourself.

I said yes to being an "honorary guest author" at a book club, *going against my gut feeling of no*, mostly because the stranger who invited me said they knew my mother (who was dead and who I missed very much). The experience turned out to be actually more like a waterboarding, where a few of the book club members, one by one, told me how little they enjoyed the memoir I had written and my life choices in general. After two hours, I finally came to my senses and excused my bewildered self. Once I reached the car, I sobbed, and it took days to process what happened. If I had trusted the no that came from my gut, I would have avoided all that pain. I could have been home instead, snuggling with my husband on the couch by the fire.

*It was the mom reference that got me.* I didn't want to disappoint my beloved mother if the person who invited me was her friend.

Lately I have been fielding requests via email or DMs from people who say things like, "I'm a friend of [very nice person who I know and admire a lot] and they said we should meet. I look forward to coffee or a Zoom call. Can't wait!"

I'm sure these people are the nicest people in the world and, in fact, maybe it's true that we should meet. But if we did meet, that's an hour that I won't have to spend with my BFF who I haven't seen in three weeks or to work on my painting (something very sacred and important to me) or to walk in the woods for an hour alone (which will transform me into a better human more capable of being present for my family).

> "Your resources are limited. You only have so much time, money, and attention at your disposal... There will always be someone who could benefit from your attention... But keep in mind, you're not responsible for solving other people's problems. You're responsible for yourself and those who depend on you (e.g., your immediate family)." —Damon Zahariades, *The Art of saying No*

# Dear Magnificent Me,

How does the idea of **prioritizing self-care** over offering service/giving care sit with you?

What requests are coming in? If you say yes, **what might you miss out on**?

# Dear Great Mystery,

Help me to **see clearly** each one of my invitations. Please show me which ones to say yes to and which ones to decline.

# I Can Unconditionally LOVE

### + have boundaries!

The boundary-setting difficulty level, for me, is often directly proportional to how much I love somebody. *With some practice*, complete strangers are a good bit easier to quickly bang off a "That won't work for me" response via email.

We all have quite a bit of practice navigating public spaces where we easily put up boundaries with strangers. When the perfume-sample lady approaches me at Macy's, for example, I no longer ever feel obligated to sniff the sample and, instead, breezily say, "No, thank you," and think nothing of it.

But, if it's my dad, a dear friend, my husband, or one of my kids? GAH! With the requests that my beloveds make of me when I am tapped-out or not particularly interested, I'm always thinking in "hit by a car terms"—as in, *I want to say no but, if I get hit by a car tomorrow and die, I would be glad that I'd said yes.*

With requests from those closest to me, each one can take on a MASSIVE LEGACY significance, i.e., *How would they remember me (after my lethal car accident...) if I refused to take them to the mall last week?* This may sound rather insane, but it's how my brain works!

This is how I ended up taking my hair-obsessed teenaged kid Charlie to Target to buy their favorite hair products last week when I was exhausted. It's also how I ended up joining a club my mom desperately wanted me to join, even though it wasn't a good fit for my personality or interests.

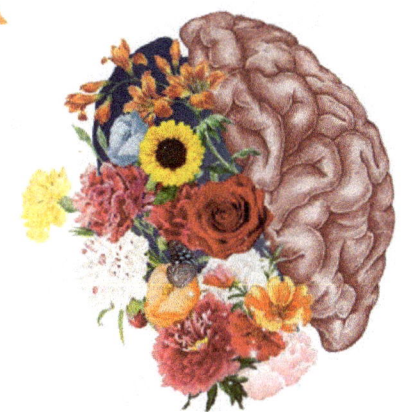

# Dear Marvelous Me,

How do you **struggle to put up boundaries** with those you love dearly?

What would it look like to love somebody unconditionally and still have boundaries that protect your **sovereignty and vitality**?

# Dear Great Mystery,

Please help me to **make and hold boundaries** that protect my well-being. Give me the **courage and strength to do it.**

# Your Compass is Here for YOU

it talks to you all the time.

Psychologist Sarri Gilman says that inside of each of us, there's an inner compass that's talking to us all the time. Our compass has an IMMEDIATE yes or a no response to every single request. The trouble is that our brains are quick to get in there and meddle with this perfect compass's reading. The trick is to be able to "hear" the quiet response that bubbles up when other parts of you (people-pleaser, inner rebel, and more) are shouting.

It's a great blessing when a request comes in that is clearly ridiculous and all parts of me are resounding together with *HELL NO!* For example, when our teenager asks, "Mom, can we go to Florida for a week and bring a few friends of mine? The weather is so bad here and we deserve a trip."

I also know that when I don't seem to be able to respond to an email for 24 hours, it's probably a no. Or, at the very least, there are boundaries that MUST be put in place. It's most commonly the case that I struggle to respond because I simply don't really want to do it, but I'm still trying to justify my no to myself.

Sometimes, I like to picture the whole thing that I'm saying yes to in full technicolor detail.

The last time I imagined saying yes, all the way to the end was when I received a request to attend an in-person book club (sheesh, you'd think I'm nearly famous in St. Louis County!) from a person who lived two hours away. She was clear that there would be no compensation but guaranteed it would be great fun. I did not know the person. I felt torn. I was so grateful for having an appreciative reader, but as I imagined getting up early on a Saturday and setting out in the car on a snowy day to travel, spending the day with strangers without getting paid, and not getting home until it was dark again, I realized it was a HECK NO.

Saying yes would have come from wanting to believe that I could control what others thought of me.

I demurred instead, and forced myself to let them think whatever they did about me, and I enjoyed my Saturday.

*No. 23*

# Dear Magnificent Me,

When was the last time you **wanted to say no but didn't**?

What or who were you **trying to control**?

What was your **immediate inner compass reading**?

If you have a people-pleaser in you, what was she trying to **convince you of**?

# Dear Great Mystery,

Please help me register **EACH AND EVERY COMPASS READING** you send me.

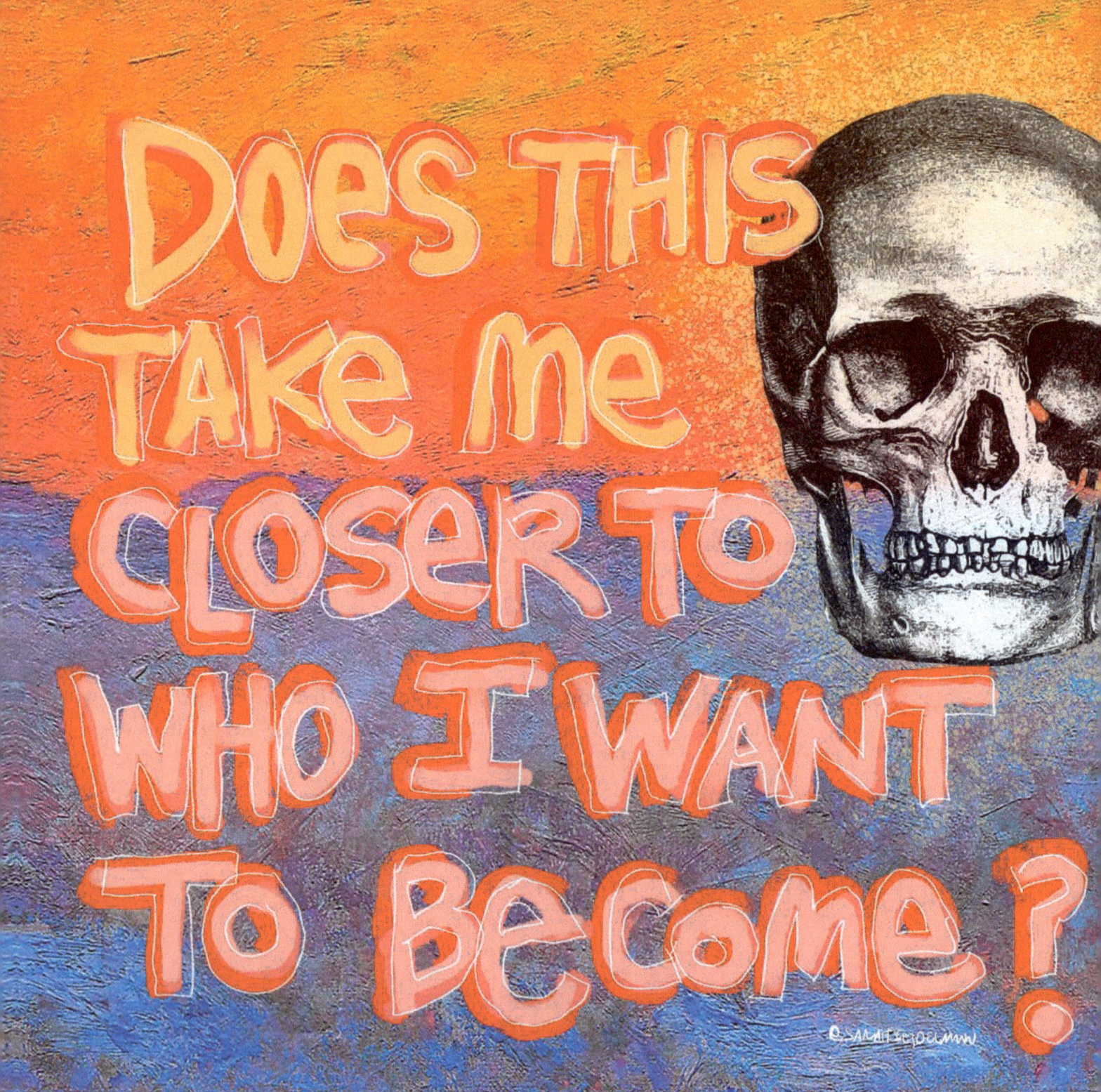

## Boundaries Shape the PERSON
*i am becoming.*

As I learn more about boundaries, it becomes clear that people with *fabulous* boundaries know who they are and where they are going! I mean, can you even imagine Maya Angelou feeling resentful and venting to her Bichon Frisé after she said yes to speaking at an event *that she has absolutely no desire to be at*? Heck no.

If each action we take is a vote for the kind of person we are becoming, it can be helpful to ask this question when you are deciding whether to say yes or no: *Does THIS take me closer to who I want to become?"*

This question can help with professional invitations, but, for me, it's also awesomely powerful when I'm tempted to break a boundary with myself.

For example, if I'm tempted to skip my morning meditation (a self-boundary I created), is that a vote for the me I want to become? Or when I want to play hooky on my two-hour writing date with myself because I'd rather scroll through the TikTok LOVESOREAL account? Heck no! I can honor myself and write first and *then* watch a few TikToks if I must.

Remembering that I'm going to die sometimes helps make boundaries clearer. *If I die tomorrow, will I be glad I said yes to this?*

# Dear Magnificent Me,

Describe the person you are **longing to become** with a few adjectives (for example: integrious, buoyant, loving, creative, confident).

Think of something you are feeling meh about that you already said yes to. What made you say yes? Be honest.

# Dear Great Mystery,

Please help me stay CLEAR ON MY HIGHEST DESTINY so that I can chose wisely as requests come in.

*No. 27*

# My Boundaries Are Hella BOUGIE

strong. over the top. extravagant.

Rhinos don't have time for everybody and everything. They are fucking rhinoceroses. They are busy being awesome.

I heard this boundary-affirming anthem from the brilliant artist Toni Jones (@iamtonijones):

> "I'm emotionally gifted so I must guard that gift with wisdom and firmness.
> My openness is emotionally generous, I must be watchful.
> I am seeing who are and aren't skilled to receive,
> I receive what others' blind spots are, teaching me about budgeting my energy
> And setting them boundaries.
> I have the right to tell people what they
> don't wanna hear in the name of
> setting them boundaries.
> I also won't exhaust myself on people who ain't listening,
> I'm done with people pleasing and attachment to making everyone happy with me.
> I love people, but my energy tolerance budget? It's hella bougie."
>
> —*Energy Budget* (song lyrics, quoted with permission)

*No. 29*

I'm reminded by this anthem that my energy is something I must guard carefully so that I have it for what's most precious to me: my beloved ones, myself, my work, and my art.

I want strong boundaries. Bougie, over the top, EXTRAvagant boundaries.

The kind that are not to be trifled with. I want to be rhino-like in this regard: armored-up with protective, self-respecting boundaries so I can be tender inside.

# Dear Magnificent Me,

**Who** do you know who has hella bougie boundaries?

Is there a page from their bougie boundaries playbook that you want to **try** on for size?

# Dear Great Mystery,

Please remind me how precious I am and show me how to courageously take up space and protect my energy when I need to.

*Me*

# CAN I TRUST

### what if i trusted there was someone else?

When I am asked by someone to do something (serve on a board, donate money to a cause, attend an event, perform a particular job, etc.), one reason I can be *tempted to say yes when I want to say no* is that: **I fear there is nobody else in the entire free world (besides *me*) who can *or is willing to* do that thing for them.** My ego shouts...

In this way, *I make saying no an impossible option*, because I imagine that my no will leave the requester in a terrible position. How can I, *the only human in the world qualified to help them*, say no? Ha! My ego can be **#totesDRAMA** like that.

*What if I trusted that there was somebody else?* Or what if I trusted that the Universe would provide the person (or company or organization) who is asking me for something with whatever they truly need? Or what if I trusted it was OK for me to rest, play, or do something else instead?

I've been learning to recognize that I am not God, and it's extremely unlikely I'm the *only one* who can help. I can choose to trust that the requester will get what they need, somehow. Eventually. And, if nobody is willing to help them, then maybe it's not meant to happen for them in that way? Something else better is coming!

# Dear Magnificent Me,

Do you ever say yes when you mean no because **you believe you are the only one** who can do that thing?

What if you trusted that **everything needed will be provided to everyone**, always? What would you **withdraw your time and support from**?

# Dear Great Mystery,

Please **help me remember who is boss** and that **my job is to focus on what I need to do to care for my very own soul**—and you will handle all the rest.

# The Hard NO

### the delivery implies the end of the conversation.

There are different flavors of "No thank you" and the more flavors you learn, the easier it gets.

This is the "hard no," as described by Sarah Knight in her brilliant book *F*ck No!*:

> "The Hard No simple, direct, and nonnegotiable. This could be a straightforward No, *a more pleasant No thank you, or a slightly more explicatory Sorry, I don't have time/can't make it/can't afford it. In any event, your content and delivery will imply that this is the end of the conversation." —Sarah Knight

I'm learning to use the "hard no" more skillfully. "I'm sorry we can't be there; we'll be out of town. When I am offered dessert or alcohol, "No, thank you" and: "No, thank you. My cardiologist had me stop all alcohol" trips off my tongue easily. That ease is hard-won and came through lots of practice and some key coaching and therapy sessions.

Recently, my brilliant friend and colleague, author Inger Kenobi, reminded me that Brené Brown says that *the opposite is true*:

Brené says this is a *fact*: **The best, *kindest*, and most loving people say no when they need to.** Her actual smarty-pants-in-a-lab research supports it.

To be more compassionate, I must say no whenever necessary.

# Dear Magnificent Me,

**Have you tried** the hard no?

Would you **like to try**?

Where could you **find support** if you could use some for help with saying no?

# Dear Great Mystery,

Please help me to be CLEAR IN MY COMMUNICATION so that my no is immediately understood and respected.

*Respect*

# I AM IMMUNE
## to your charms.

When I worked long hours at the hospital all the time, boundaries with my young children were *so hard* for me. Because I felt so much guilt for barely being home, I wanted to say yes to every request they made of me.

I began to develop a pattern where I'd say yes ("We can make cupcakes *and* go to the zoo on Mommy's Day off!") and then I'd have to back-pedal part of the promise (or, sometimes, all of it). Frequently, I was too exhausted, or we had other stuff that needed doing instead, like grocery shopping.

Did I mention how charming my children are? Each of them was masterful at getting me to say yes. One had the whole *Puss in Boots* (from SHREK) "big, sad eyes" trick down. Others would snuggle with me quietly and then launch their request (affection is my Love Language). I was putty in their hands!

Naturally, the kids would get extremely disappointed when I would change my mind about the zoo or cupcakes. It got to the point where they no longer trusted me, and I didn't trust me either.

After observing that distressing (for all of us) pattern of promising and back pedaling for a while, I finally made a new policy: "When Mommy says yes, mommy means yes. And when Mommy says no, Mommy means no." And that policy got me to stop promising crazy things *right quick*. There were slip ups for sure but my boundary with them and with me made a huge difference at home.

**I AM NOT PERFECT.** I'm not perfect. Even today, when my kids ask me to go do something (they are now 18 to 26 years old), I frequently want to (and do) drop everything to say yes to them. I am still learning to check in with myself first.

**STILL LEARNING...** Kids are hard to refuse, and don't get me started with pugs. Saying no to a pug who wants food (when it's not suppertime) can feel nearly impossible. These days, I'm practicing walking out of the kitchen when Oliver James is working me over with his sad pug eyes.

Oprah says to remember what yes feels like—all the way to the consequences. Like when the veterinarian weighs Oliver and asks me who's in charge of portioning his food. I will have to confess, It's me!

# Dear Magnificent Me,

**Who are you most likely to break your own boundaries for?** Is it your Siberian Husky, your über charming children, grandchildren, or somebody else?

What sort of policy with yourself (and others) could you create to **rebuild your own integrity** boundary by boundary?

# Dear Great Mystery,

Please help me to stay in integrity with myself by saying yes to commitments only when I have the energy and capacity to follow through on them.

# BOUNDARIES
## Make Love Possible
### boundaries create sacred space.

My boundaries are the fences and walls (at times, they must be 16-inch thick cement reinforced with rebar) that I must put up in my work life and private life if I'm to have the capacity to love—myself and others.

This image of a stone house popped up as I was searching for a way to express this truth about boundaries. It became the inspiration for the art I created to the left. Boundaries literally contain and corral the love in my life. Like the walls of a wonderful home, boundaries create sacred space so that I can feel safe and protected... it's soul physics. And home is such a beautiful metaphor for what is intimate and most precious: shelter, a place to rest, a safe space, space to be creative.

Like actual fences and walls, boundaries don't stay up forever. Dogs can dig holes under them. Trees fall on them. People drive drunk into them. Storms may weaken or damage them. Maintenance will be required of our boundaries.

LOVE

> We cannot expect others to mend our disrespected boundaries or to understand the reasons we must have them in the first place.
>
> **THAT'S OUR JOB**

# Dear Magnificent Me,

If your life were a home, **what sort of walls would you need right now** to create some space for yourself?

Is there an existing boundary you made in the past, either with yourself or with another person, that **needs repair or shoring up?**

# Dear Great Mystery,

Please **help me to create needed boundaries** and to maintain the ones already in place.

*Maintain*

# Boundaries Are an Act of REVERENCE

### nobody wants to be a groaner! let's be noble instead.

I don't know about you, but for me, thinking of my boundaries as holy (as in, they help me to be able to serve the Great Mystery at a higher level) is an extremely motivating idea.

What if you maintained your boundaries as an act of reverence for you and, ultimately, for the gift of life, for that power greater than yourself—the Universe, God, Mother Earth, or whatever you call that creative force? Here's why this approach is solid.

To refuse to create and/or tend to your boundaries is to invite:
- **Loss of respect** from self and others.
- **Loss of control** of the direction of your life.
- **Increased chaos**, distractions, and guilt.
- **Loss of interest** in life itself.
- **Unmet goals** and the stress of chaos, which can lead to hopelessness, depression, or anxiety.

Without your willingness to uphold personal boundaries,

> "You will act, sleep, work, groan, feel used and fulfill basic responsibilities rather than make choices to live and love fully, to work hard and nobly, to fulfill your purpose and to contribute passionately to your world." —J. Black and G. Enns, *Better Boundaries*

Nobody wants to be a groaner! Let's be noble instead.

# Dear Magnificent Me,

What or who do you treat with **great reverence**? (For example: nature. I'm in awe of nature and constantly giving thanks for its beauty and largesse.) What would it look like to use the same approach of reverence toward **your own life**?

What boundary would you **immediately** put up (or reinstate)? (For example: I would give gratitude to myself regularly—weird idea! And I would make sure my calendar time for creating art or wandering in the woods was not flexible. I would treat it like an appointment with Michelle Obama. No way am I asking Michelle to reschedule!)

# Dear Great Mystery,

Please help me remember that creating and upholding my boundaries ensures that I have the capacity to be IN SERVICE to you and my fellow humans and beasties.

# How Far Would You GO to protect yourself?

Author Elizabeth Gilbert (of *Eat, Pray Love* fame) is one of my very favorite thinkers and is a master of boundaries. She told a story* about just how far she would go to protect her own boundaries.

Her partner Raya was dying of pancreatic cancer and, as addicts sometimes do, Raya relapsed back into drug addiction as her death approached. Instead of sucking it up, or simply being compassionate with Raya in her darkest hour, Liz did something I did not expect. She asked Raya to find a sober-ish moment so they could speak when she wasn't too high. Then Liz lovingly explained to Raya that she was no longer able to take care of her if she was going to continue to use drugs, and that she would be leaving to take care of herself.

I don't know about you, but that choice worried me! I mean, aren't we supposed to be super compassionate with the dying? No matter what?

Well, Liz left. Raya immediately moved back in with her ex, who was well familiar with Raya's addiction and helped her get sober once last time. Once Raya was sober again, she called Liz, who then returned to help (along with Raya's ex) and support Raya as she died.

Wow. It could have ended differently, of course. But the bottom line was that Liz was willing to be kind to herself. She knew that living with active addiction was not being kind to herself.

*Podcast episode: "Liz Gilbert Shares the Whole Story for the First Time" on We Can Do Hard Things, with Glennon Doyle," Episode 94:

# Dear Magnificent Me,

What does this story make you **feel**?

How far might you go to protect your own boundaries with the **vulnerable, the addicted, the sick and the dying**?

# Dear Great Mystery,

Please give me the COURAGE TO MAKE HEALTHY BOUNDARIES, even with those who are addicted, sick, infirm, or vulnerable.

*Courage*

# It's NOT Everyone's Job
## to understand your calling.

When others give us unsolicited advice about our life path it often hurts. A lot. One of the toughest boundaries I've ever had to set was with my mom.

When I was attempting to move from being a physician (a well-respected profession, in my mom's eyes) to becoming a life coach (a frequently misunderstood vocation with variable degrees of respect in our culture), my mom was afraid for me and said some discouraging things to keep me "safe" from making that leap. That was such a difficult time for me and knowing my mom disapproved of my choices made it more so.

So, we must *boundary-up* when we are making these choices that come from our very soul. *Nobody else can make these boundaries for us.* We must live with the outcomes of our choices of career, whether we lease or own our car, the partner we choose, the way we parent our kids, the food we eat, the adventures we choose.

Our life choices are *prime* boundary territory. Nobody but us can determine the best path for ourselves.

# Dear Magnificent Me,

Who has challenged your boundaries by questioning **your unique life choices**?

Is there somebody in your life who you wish would make a **different life choice**?

What would it look like if you radically **accepted their choices** (and honored that boundary)?

# Dear Great Mystery,

Please give me the courage to FOLLOW TO MY OWN INNER VOICE for all of my decisions and to protect it by placing boundaries around my choices.

# Boundaries With ADDICTS *and more.*

The word *Addict* in this illustration could be replaced by *person struggling with mental illness*, or *personality disorder* or *chronic disease/chronic pain*.

Here's what Melody Beattie says about this in her book *Codependent No More*:

> For some of us, the idea that we were responsible for other people's feelings had its roots in childhood and was established by members of our nuclear family. We may have been told that we made our mother or father miserable, leading directly to the idea that we were also responsible for making them happy. The idea that we are responsible for our parents' happiness or misery can instill exaggerated feelings of power and guilt in us.
>
> We do not have this kind of power over our parents - over their feelings, or over the course of their lives. We do not have to allow them to have this kind of power over us." -Melody Beattie

My younger sister Maria struggled with depression when we were young, and I remember feeling guilty that I felt so good. It didn't seem fair. I wanted to try to "fix her" in my own eleven-year-old way. As a young adult I desperately wanted her to get better, so she wouldn't have to suffer. Healing from co-dependency means letting people experience whatever they are experiencing. You can be present for someone without trying to fix or heal them.

In the case of an adult addict, we let them experience the natural consequences of their own actions, rather than trying to protect them from the consequences.

## Signs of a Codependent Relationship
Source: WomensHealthMag.com

- You take too much responsibility for your partner (or adult child, parent or friend.)
- You gravitate toward people who need you.
- You never get your way.
- They've told you that you're a "nag".
- You'd describe your partner (or adult child, parent, friend etc) as immature.
- You only fight about one thing.
- You do things for them that they should do on their own.
- You talk about their issues more than your own.
- You struggle to identify your own emotions.
- You check in with your partner (or adult child, parent or friend) before doing anything.

## 10 Signs You're in a Codependent Relationship
Source: ClevelandClinic.org

- You feel like you need to save them from themselves.
- You want to change who they are.
- Taking time out for self-care makes you feel selfish.
- It's difficult to explain how you're feeling about your relationship.
- You feel anxious when you don't hear from them.
- You have trouble being alone. You routinely cancel plans to be with them.
- Your space doesn't feel like it's yours.
- You feel like maybe you ask for too much.
- Their behavior escalates when you try to set healthy boundaries.

# Dear Magnificent Me,

**Do you feel responsible** for anybody's suffering? Whose?

**How is that impacting your relationship(s)** and what boundary might be helpful?

# Dear Great Mystery,

Please help me allow other people to **be as they** are without trying to change, heal, or fix them.
Help me to STAY IN MY LANE
and let you do
the heavy lifting.

*No. 55*

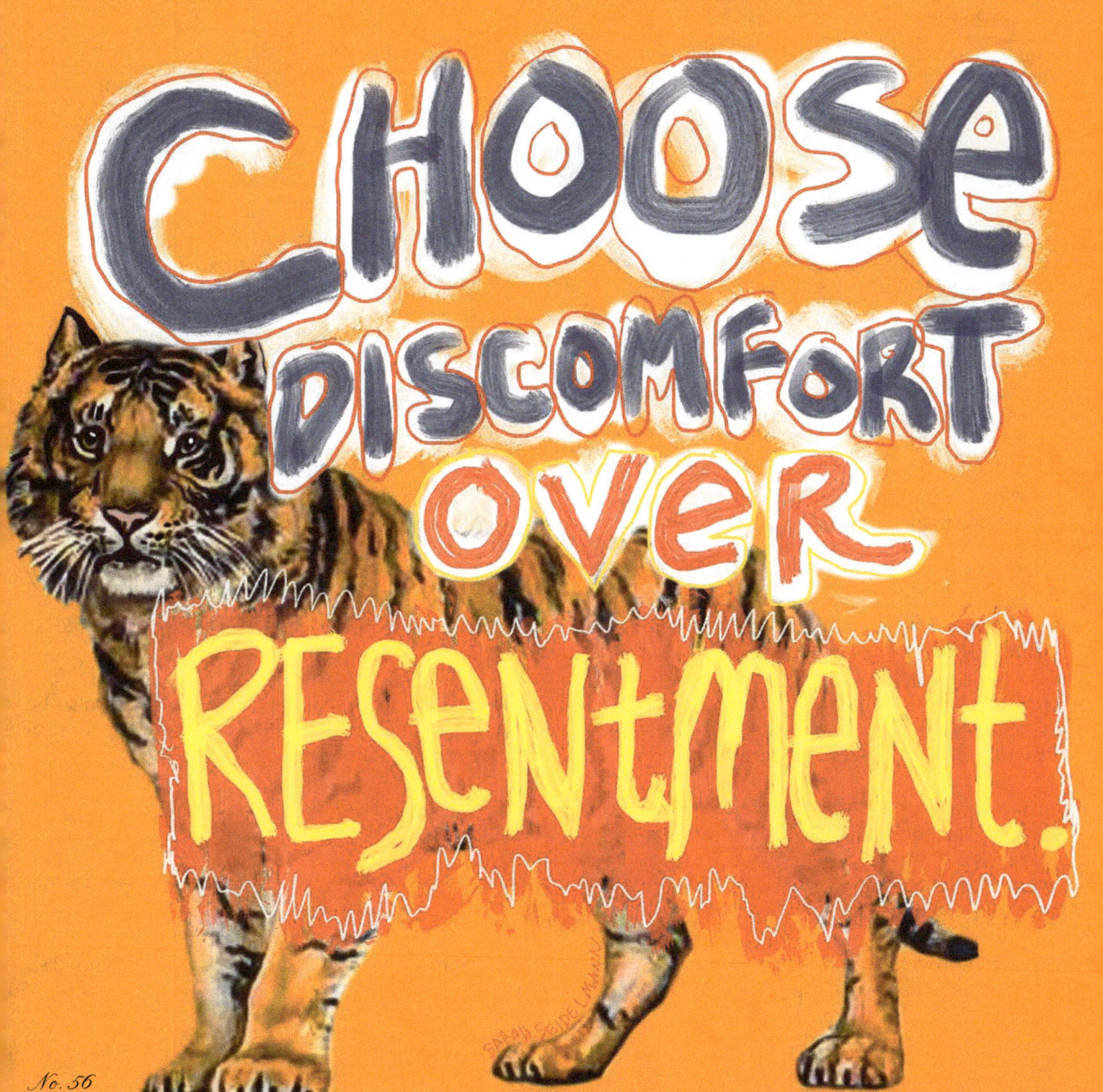

# CHOOSE DISCOMFORT OVER resentment.

The hardest thing is not *setting the boundary*. The *hard* thing is facing the reaction of the person we set it with. Can I be OK even if they are mad, sad, disappointed?

One of the things I learned while among my fellow food addicts in a twelve-step program is that I cannot afford a resentment. When I am resentful, I am infinitely more likely to "eat" over it. So, I have to choose discomfort if I want to stay conscious and not end up in the ditch, foodwise. My own history tells me that my boundary-setting will disappoint others.

For example, in 2011 I decided to set a boundary to take care of my weary self and step down from a board after five years of service. Watching the director's face fall and hearing the stinging disappointment in her voice was *so hard*. I didn't want her to feel unsupported.

In 2005, I decided to get rid of a rocking chair that my mom had given to us (she didn't want it at her house any longer). The rocker was not comfy. When you rocked, you felt as if you might flip back completely and get a head injury. It was unnerving. When my mom learned that I was getting rid of the chair, she got upset. She had an attachment to me enjoying it.

If I cave into the discomfort of other people's feelings and try to fix them, I will feel resentful. I will also be immediately at risk for commencing to eat way too many pieces of what I like to call *not my food* (NMF), because I cannot get enough of it to fill the anxiety-ridden, guilt-ridden or resentment-laden hole in my soul.

Putting up boundaries has *never* felt smooth or cool or effortless to me, *ever*. But the feeling after setting the boundary and getting the payoff is *incredible*.

**Payoff after stepping off the board:** I finally had the little extra spaciousness I needed to tend to myself, my family, and my dreams. It was like I'd gotten a 100-pound gorilla off my back.

**Payoff after releasing the rocking chair:** I had more space in my family room for a chair that somebody could sit in to rest their hooves and read. Mom and I laughed about it (later!).

*No. 57*

# Dear Magnificent Me,

Have you ever overeaten, gotten drunk, overexercised, used drugs, shopped, gambled, or used sex **to numb the feeling of resentment**?

Looking back, when have you set a boundary and gotten a **fabulous payoff**? (Hint: It can be small.)

Where do you currently need the **courage to be uncomfortable** so that you can set a much-needed boundary?

# Dear Great Mystery,

Please give me the courage to sit with discomfort, and remind me that the feelings of others will pass.

# CO-DEPENDENCY

is being overly invested in the feelings or outcomes of other people in your life to the detriment of your own feelings + outcomes.

— Terri Cole "Boundary Boss"

# CO-DEPENDENCY
## it's time to unlearn it.

I've done a lot of recovery from co-dependency (thank you, Al-Anon and Melody Beattie!), and I'm still unlearning these ways.

I was indoctrinated by my culture and, to some extent, by my family, as a girl/young woman *to take care of the feelings of everyone.* Co-dependency hits me hardest at home.

Anne Lamott says that becoming a parent can feel like living with "your heart outside of your body" for the rest of your life. I love my kids so damn much, so it's hard for me when I perceive that they are suffering or having trouble. The same goes with my partner Mark, my parents (when they were alive), and all my BFFs.

But if I get so wrapped up and "concerned" for them that I am no longer able to enjoy my own life, I'm in trouble. This is the essence of co-dependency.

I've also heard co-dependency defined as "the need to look to another person to *know* how we feel." So, if they are miserable, so are we. I'm sure you can tell how insane that sounds.

Here's what has helped me to extricate myself from the unfortunate swamp of co-dependency:

> Remembering that I am not God. I am not here to fix everyone's problems. I am here to bear witness. I believe that each person has their own Higher Power and guardian angels and is being guided each step of the way. When I worry or fret about others, *I am actively doubting the Great Mystery's ability to care for them.* And that is truly riDONCulous. Surely the great power that made pugs and peonies has got the situation handled.
>
> I am learning to be truly OK when you are not OK. **I can feel my own feelings, but if I must feel yours too, we are both in trouble.**

Here's my favorite Hafiz (a Sufi poet) poem for co-dependency:

"**Troubled?** Stay with me, for I am not. When I am at peace, no matter what's happening for other people, I can be a force for good."

# Dear Magnificent Me,

Whose moods (or circumstances/behaviors/choices) are most likely to send you into a **tizzy**?

What approach would help you **remain peaceful**, no matter what is going on in the lives of that person?

# Dear Great Mystery,

Please help me to be untroubled, no matter what situations or circumstances may befall by beloveds.
Help me to be present for them and
BEAR WITNESS without fixing.

# RESPECT YOUR self.

re·spect, /ri-'spekt/ (noun) – "a feeling of deep admiration for someone or something elicited by their abilities, qualities, or achievements" —*Merriam-Webster Dictionary*

A lot of my reading and exploring about boundaries has led to this: Having *stone cold solid boundaries* (and maintaining them) is ultimately the proof that we do, in fact, respect ourselves. If I don't respect myself enough to say no, hold up my own boundaries, or ask for what I need, how will anybody else respect me? Here's an opportunity for you to check in and find that nugget of self-respect—ask yourself:

*Do I have deep admiration for myself?*

Weirdly, that's something I have never asked myself before. As I sit with this, I can answer yes. In many ways, I do have deep admiration for myself.

### Dear Magnificent Me,

**What do you deeply admire about yourself**, your qualities, or your achievements?

### Dear Great Mystery,
### Please help me to develop my respect for myself. Show me where I shine
### so that I can have the courage to develop healthy boundaries.

*No. 63*

# PROTECT
## Your Space  do it for well-being, sanity, or safety.

Setting boundaries with those we perceive as vulnerable can feel heartbreaking, even when we know we must do it for our own well-being, sanity, or safety.

When I asked my friends for their stories of boundaries, one friend told me about his father, who had abandoned their family twenty years ago to pursue a life that was terribly unstable. One day, the father showed up in my friend's hometown, desperately needing shelter and some support. Despite the years that had passed, my friend lovingly helped his father find suitable housing he could afford and co-signed the lease. He knew he couldn't allow his dad (with his chaotic lifestyle) to live with him in his own home.

Six months later, his father left town without notice. His father didn't return and got behind on his rent. My friend began getting phone calls from the rental agency. Eventually, he had to put up a boundary with his father by deciding not to bail him out. His dad got evicted. My friend knew his father was not interested in pursuing a life of stability and safety. Even though his father's mental health was not good, my friend realized that trying to fix his father was ultimately damaging his own mental health and sense of peace. That was the hardest boundary he'd ever had to make. He did it with the support of a therapist.

**WE CAN LOVE PEOPLE WHO ARE ADDICTED**

We can love people who are addicted, mentally ill, abusive, or those we perceive as vulnerable without supporting them financially, letting them live in our homes, being in their physical presence, or trying to fix or repair the circumstances they find themselves in. Sometimes we must do this to preserve our own well-being or safety. Setting boundaries with those we perceive as vulnerable can feel heartbreaking, even when we know we must do it for our own well-being, sanity, or safety.

# Dear Magnificent Me,

Have you ever had to make a boundary with a loved one who you believed was vulnerable to **protect yourself**?

**Where do you overextend yourself** when you perceive that another person is vulnerable?

What would a **good** boundary look like?

# Dear Great Mystery,

Please remind me that you are always caring for everyone and everything. Help me to tend to MY OWN NEEDS FIRST so that I might truly be of service to you.

*Me First*

# Irritation Is a SIGN of a boundary violation.

After my beautiful mom died in 2020, I decided to invest in ten sessions of Internal Family Systems (IFS) parts work for myself. Losing a parent felt primal for me, and I felt my mom's spirit encouraging me to be more generous with myself.

During one of those wonderful IFS sessions, I shared that I had felt a weird burst of anger when somebody hadn't shown up for a complimentary consultation call. I had been working really hard that summer with hardly a break and felt extremely irritated when that person was a no-show. I was also still grieving mom's death.

The IFS therapist said, "Sounds like a boundary thing. Anger is often a sign that our boundaries have been breached."

And, suddenly, I realized that things needed to change. I needed a new way of working with clients.

My old boundaries around "complimentary consultations" had been set when I first was launching my coaching practice. It had been over ten years since then and I was extremely busy at the moment. I no longer needed to offer free fifteen-minute consults anymore. In fact, I discovered that I needed to raise my rates to gain a modicum of sanity in my schedule.

> Nobody had ever told me that anger is a sign that you may be dealing with a boundary issue.
>
> I raised my rates, removed the "free consult" option from my website, and soon my practice was feeling so much better.
>
> Boundaries are living, breathing entities that need to change over time. What worked ten years ago may needed to be upleveled now.

 # Dear Magnificent Me,

Where might you need to review and **uplevel your boundaries**?

When were you **last** irritated?

**How** might your boundaries have been involved?

 # Dear Great Mystery,

Please help me to identify the true cause of my irritation & anger so that I may change the things I can.

WHEN YOU SAY YES, BUT YOU MEAN NO— that's not being kind, that's being DISHONEST.

SARAH SEIDELMANN

# DISHONEST
## Let's Pay Attention and be honest about our boundaries.

Sharks are beautiful beasties and they tend to make us pay attention, which is why I chose one for this illustration. Let's pay attention and be *honest* about our boundaries.

In a research study*, people were asked to carry out tasks that went against their ethics. Although they voiced their objections, half the subjects agreed to deface a library book. That was because saying no felt too difficult.

Martha Beck's incredible book, *The Way of Integrity*, has a lot to say on this topic. It's so hard for us to truly be honest in every aspect of our lives because we live in a society where we are taught to be *polite*.

On a recent podcast**, Martha referenced research that was done. In "this one study, they said to some people, 'Just don't lie quite as much for a couple of weeks.' They had no way of policing it. They just suggested this. At the end of those weeks, the people who had lied less than the control group had fewer physical symptoms of illness. They had fewer doctor visits, they had better relationship quality going on. They had a better time at their work. Everything started to feel better when they just started checking to see what was true for them, and then staying with what was true for them instead of selling themselves out again."

It truly is painful to lie or to be out of integrity with ourselves. It causes physical and emotional suffering. I hope that motivates you to stop selling yourself out and to speak your boundaries courageously!

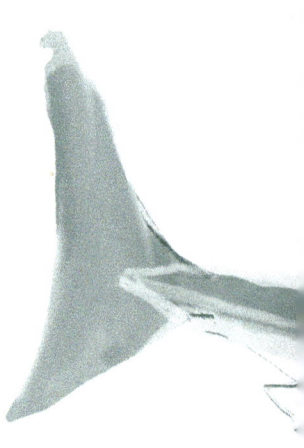

*No. 71*

*Underestimating Our Influence Over Others' Unethical Behavior and Decisions* Vanessa K. Bohns, M. Mahdi Roghanziad & Amy Z. Xu, University of Waterloo, Waterloo, Ontario, Canada. Published in *Personality and Social Psychology Bulletin*.

**Podcast Episode: "Living without Lying (Martha Beck PhD)" on Pulling the Thread, with Elise Loehnen.

# Dear Magnificent Me,

Have you experienced **illness or physical discomfort** because you failed to have a healthy boundary around a situation?

How could you approach that **same situation but with a boundary**?

# Dear Great Mystery,

Please help me to take care of myself—body, mind, and soul—by setting healthy boundaries.

*Myself*

No. 72

# I'M NOT able to do that.

I listened to an interview of Shonda Rhimes by Oprah. Shonda shared that these are the words she relies on to decline invitations: "No I'm not able to do that."

Shonda used to offer up explanations for why she was unable to do the thing (whatever it was), but she no longer does. She realized that, in giving reasons, she was trying to defend her "niceness," or to "prove" that she had a legitimate reason for saying no.

She said it was hard to stop doing that and she lost few friends over it, but ultimately it was freeing. She got happier. She's not doing anything she doesn't want to be doing any more. Shonda on saying no:

> "So, I decide to treat saying no in the same way I treat saying thank you. Say no and then don't say anything else. I came up with three different clear ways of saying no.
>
> **1** I am not going to be able to do that. **2** That is not going to work for me. **3** And there's simply: No."
>
> —Shonda Rhimes, *Year of Yes*

When we are starting out with boundaries, we need to explore different scripts and ways of saying no. Here are some options:

Sadly, I have something else at that time.
I'm afraid I can't.
I'm honored you asked me, but I simply can't.
I'm sorry I'm not able to fit it in.
Unfortunately, I already have plans.
I don't have the bandwidth for that right now.
I have another commitment.

— Erin Eatough, "How to Say No to Others (and Why You Shouldn't Feel Guilty)," Better Up Blog.

# Dear Magnificent Me,

Who do you know who says no to you **in a way that feels good to you** (even though none of us love hearing a no)?

When you need to **say no to someone**, what would it look like?

# Dear Great Mystery,

Please help me to find feel-good ways for me to decline invitations so that I may truly thrive and SHINE IN THIS LIFE.

No. 75

# Never Say NO without a number.

This boundary idea is a little different and has to do with work opportunities. I am not even sure this is a boundary, but it feels like such an important idea for creatives and entrepreneurs that I'm including it.

The tip comes from my sister!!!
## Maria Bamford
who is an amazing comedian!!!
with her own Netflix show!!!!!!!!

Let's say somebody offers you some sort of work (or contract job) and you initially think to yourself, *no way, no how am I doing that!*

You are about to put up a boundary *because you predict or believe what they will offer you monetarily will be insufficient*—you think they aren't going to pay you enough to do this sort of work or this project.

Maria learned this tip from her fellow comedian Jackie Kashian, who's dad sold aluminum siding for part of his life. Here's his advice in such a situation: "Never say no without a number."

So, *before you reflexively say no*, think of a payment number (however ridiculous) for which you'd be happy to do the work. Of course, if *no* amount of cash would bring you into integrity with yourself for this job, then forget about it and say no.

The caveat is that if they agree to your terms, you'll have to say yes!

My sister has employed this strategy many times, with delightful and surprising success.

# Dear Magnificent Me,

Have you ever wanted to reflexively say no because **you assumed** the terms you would be offered would not be good?

**Are you willing to try this strategy** to "never say no without a number" in your professional life?

# Dear Great Mystery,

Please remind me **not to leap** to conclusions about any invitations. Help me slow my roll and explore options.

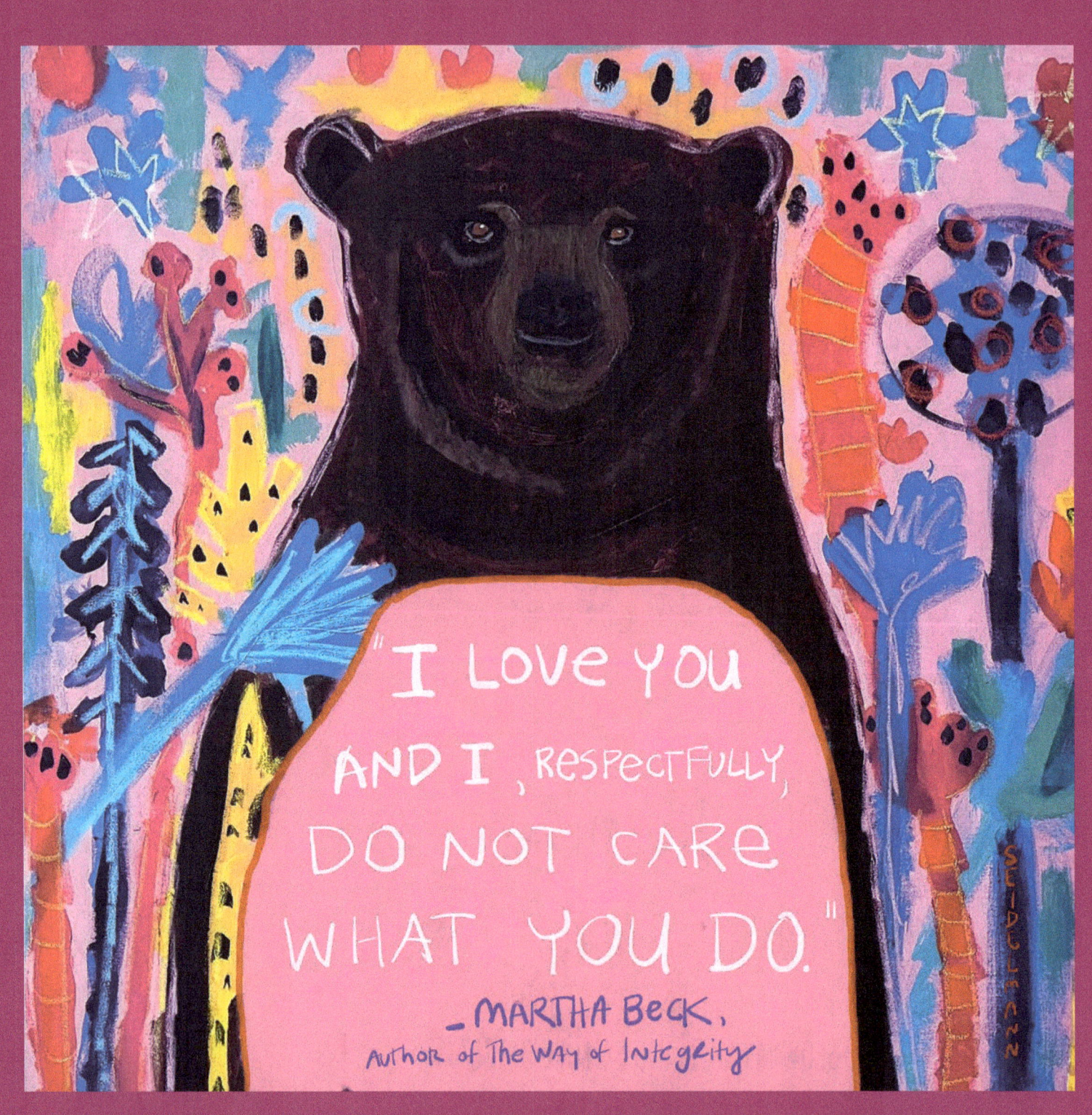

# I LOVE you.

If we want better boundaries, we *also* need to also practice *honoring the boundaries of others*.

This line (illustrated above) comes from Martha Beck and it's handy when, say, your 29-year-old daughter comes home for the holidays and announces that she's selling everything and moving to India to enter an ashram for the rest of her life. You are welcome to visit, she tells you, but she's not coming back home, ever.

In that moment, you are likely feeling stunned, hurt, mystified, and more. But if you truly want to respect the hell out of your adult child's boundaries, you will quickly say to them (while looking them in the eye), "I love you and I, respectfully, do not care what you do."

This line can sound so cold to the uninitiated, but it's a boundary-safeguarding *treasure*. My life goal is to truly live this way!

Imagine the future of your relationship if you tried to talk your daughter out of going to India, if you got angry, or took it all personally (*My daughter's choice to live in India permanently means she doesn't care about me*).

Can you imagine how that might make your daughter feel?

I use this line from Martha frequently with my clients, like when they ask me, "Should I quit this job and take the other one?" or "Am I a horrible person for wanting to move away from my husband's family?"

Ultimately, each sovereign adult must decide for themselves what the right move is for them, and if we love and care about them, we will detach and let them go.

DETACH AND LET THEM GO

# Dear Magnificent Me,

**How** do you react to this line of Martha's and this idea?

Have you ever withheld love or judged another adult loved one **because of a choice they made?**

# Dear Great Mystery,

Please help me to **stay in my lane** today and always.

# I AM BLENDING to quiet me.

One "sign" that you might have a boundary problem is, as Annie Wright says:

> "You're a chameleon. You tend to lose yourself in relationships. You become who and what the other person wants and needs you to be – in personality, preference, temperament, and even appearance – and you tend to merge and take on the preferences and characteristics of the other person. This is a sign your relational boundaries may need work."
> –Annie Wright, Relational Trauma Recovery Specialist

I think some chameleon-ing is natural. As an empathic human, I naturally try to align with others when I am in their presence. I'm sensitive to their political beliefs, religion, life choices, etc., as I converse with them. I may not bring up a topic that is precious to me that I believe would not sit well with them.

I am also aware that being in integrity, for me, also means showing up as the *same exact* me in all spaces that I enter.

I don't need to shrink or get larger, quiet my opinions, or manipulate anybody when I am connected to my essential self.

I AM CONNECTED TO MY ESSENTIAL SELF

# Dear Magnificent Me,

Is there a place or a human that **triggers you into believing** that you are not acceptable "as is," where you feel less-than, or possibly greater-than (the ego is good for that!?)

What would it look like if you showed up **just as you are**?

# Dear Great Mystery,

Please remind me in every moment that I am OK just as I am. I do not need to conform to anybody else's standards.

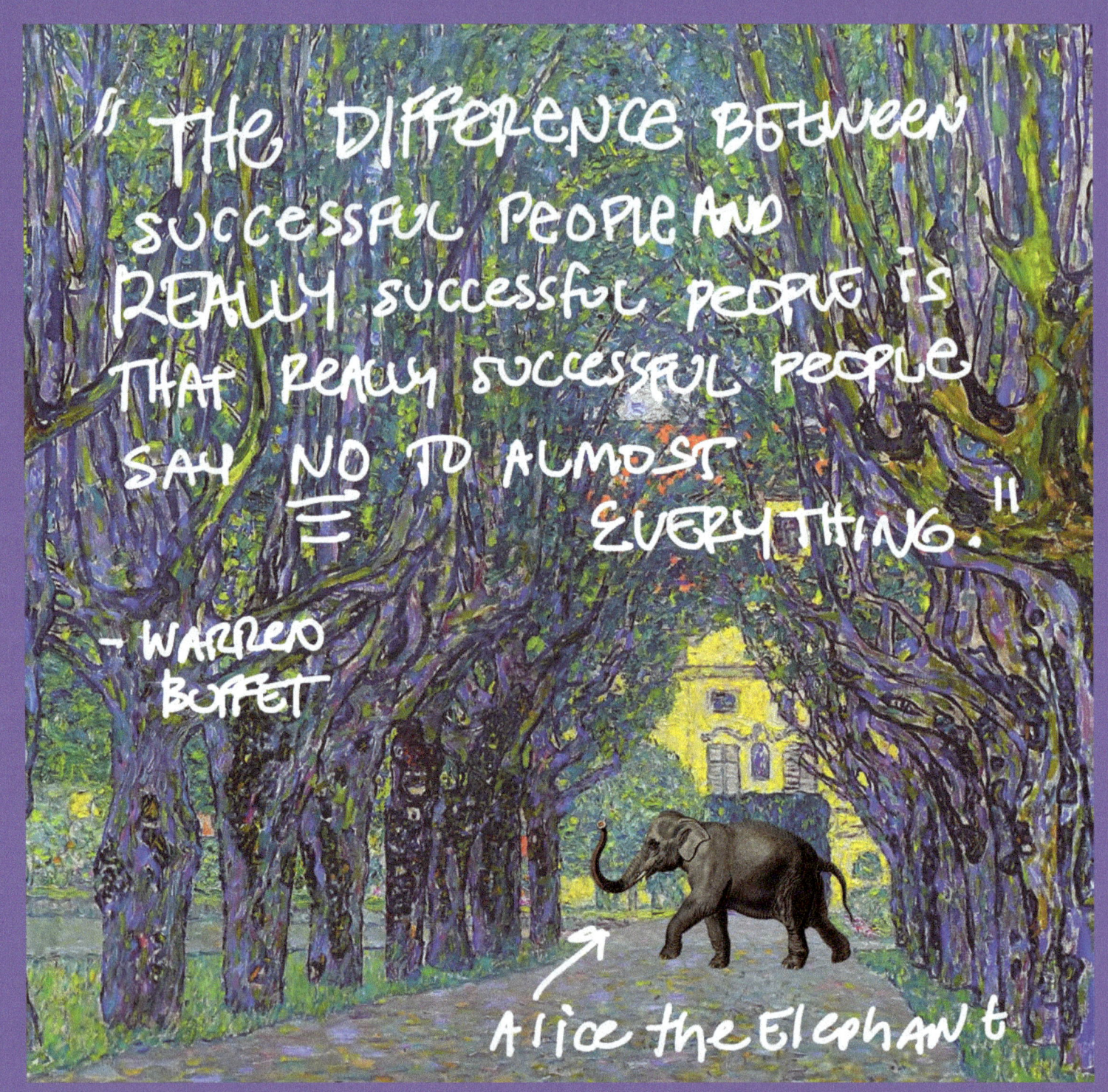

# Really Successful People Say NO

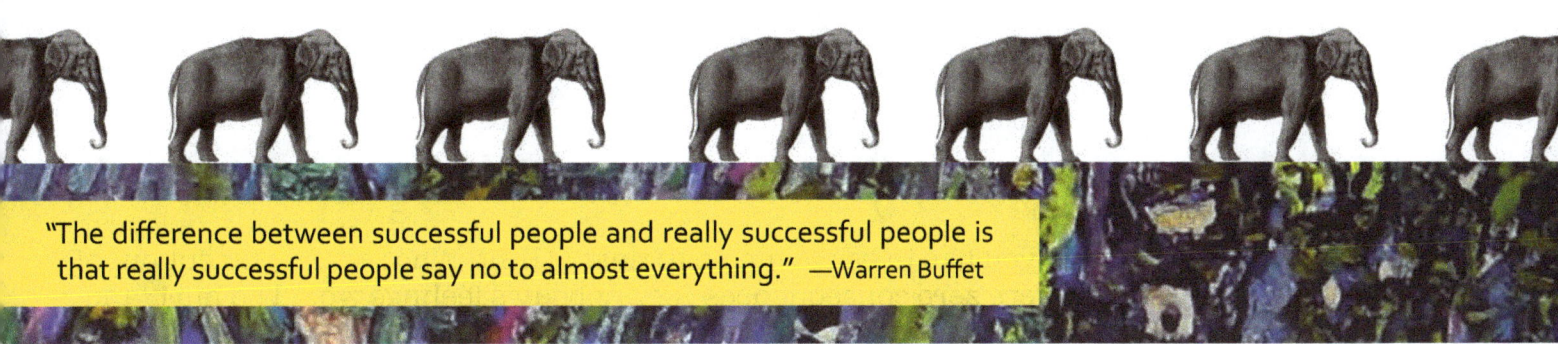

"The difference between successful people and really successful people is that really successful people say no to almost everything." —Warren Buffet

Every time I've seen this quote *it stops me in my tracks* and I marvel for a moment at the confidence and clarity it would take to say no to almost everything. And, for that matter, to be so certain what *is* and what *is not* something I want or need to get involved with. I fantasize about how simple my life could be if I were this sort of person! And I wonder if the kind of "success" I'm after may be vastly different from the world of Warren Buffet. Or maybe it's not?

Years ago, I officially joined a group that had lots of history. I did it with complete awareness that I joined for the purpose of making my mom happy. Mom was happy enough, but me joining the group really pleased her. And I wanted to please her. Badly. A few years later, my mom died unexpectedly after an illness that lasted two-and-a-half years. Boy, was I glad I had said yes to joining that thing that wasn't necessarily my "thing," because my mom and I got to do it together.

So, I believe learning to say yes and no to things is complicated. There are a million things I am so grateful I've learned to say no to, especially (but not limited to):

**Donating to organizations that aren't aligned with my values** (and being able to say yes to those that are).

**Attending pyramidal marketing parties** (Mary Kay, Amway, and all the others). If I like a product, I can always purchase it without attending a party about it.

**Requests from strangers on the Internet** to "pick my brain."

# Dear Magnificent Me,

What have you started saying no to with **ease**?

What more would you like to be saying no to **now**? (Hint: What would you cut out of your life if there were zero consequences (i.e., nobody's feelings would be hurt, and you'd still go to heaven and everybody would be awesome)?

# Dear Great Mystery,

Please help me connect with my divine Self and HEAR THAT SOFT VOICE THAT SAYS, NO THANK YOU AND HEED ITS REQUEST.

# Boundaries Are the PATH to self respect.

Boundaries aren't about love restriction—they are *really* about self-love and self-regard.

When we love ourselves, it naturally gives others permission to love themselves. Yay! So... why do I so easily forget to regard myself when I am *right here*?

Self-*respect*. *Respect of the self*. I feel like I need to type that out a few times. *Respect of the self. Respect of me.*

As a young girl and as a woman, I've felt like self-respect was not something I learned from society. Instead, I learned obedience, performance (Smile! Be kind!) and keeping the peace. I was so afraid of being rejected or unloved, or of not belonging. No wonder I've hesitated to put up boundaries my whole life.

As I have grown up a little bit, I've enacted more boundaries, with growing confidence. For example, I've learned to say, "I'm not able to do that. However, I would love to share another resource with you." And "I'm busy working on a creative project and prioritizing my client work and I'm unable to meet with you." And "Thank you so much for asking! I decided last year to stop doing that kind of work, so I must decline. Have you thought about asking [some another person who might be truly interested/available]?"

Respect of the self. Respect of me.
Respect of the self. Respect of me.
Respect of the self. Respect of me.
Respect of the self. Respect of me.
Respect of the self. Respect of me.
Respect of the self. Respect of me.
Respect of the self. Respect of me.
Respect of the self. Respect of me.
Respect of the self. Respect of me.
Respect of the self. Respect of me.
Respect of the self. Respect of me.
Respect of the self. Respect of me.

# Dear Magnificent Me,

Is there a part of you that **worries** that if you put up a boundary would mean that you have a giant wall around your heart?

If so, try this prompt, filling in the blank: "If I were full of **loving self-respect**, I would create a boundary with [person]."

# Dear Great Mystery,

Please help me to respect myself in all places and with all people. Show me how to show myself that I matter and that my well-being is important to SAFEGUARD.

Lack of boundories invites a lack of respect.

— ANONYMOUS

# Lack of Boundaries Invites LACK of respect.

My very first life coach was Michelle (from mylifecoach.com) and I still remember her saying to me (back in 2008), "Sarah, you teach people how to treat you."

Wow. I didn't even know what that meant. I wrote it down several times. I found it confusing. All those years of medical training, and mostly what I had learned was that my life was not my own.

Sarah in medical school/residency: "I'll do what you tell me to do, no matter what I think or feel about it."

Sometimes, the things I was asked to do in medical school felt so bad that I did speak up. I remember watching a patient get sicker and sicker each day until I realized that the resident wasn't even rounding on my patient. That neglect was having serious consequences for the patient who was becoming more ill each day. I finally approached the resident and begged her to see the patient. She rebuffed me and later I was reprimanded by the chair of the department for "trying to be one of the chiefs and not one of the Indians." I felt helpless and angry. No wonder I stopped wanting to speak up. I didn't feel respected.

**ASK FOR WHAT YOU NEED**

# Dear Magnificent Me,

What would it look like for you to teach people how to treat you? **Who do you most need to teach?**

Is there a place where your actions show that you respect others more than you respect yourself? What do you predict would happen if you **brought in more self-respect**?

# Dear Great Mystery,

Please show me how to love and respect myself so that I may walk in this world full of the POWER of my own soul.

# I HAVE THE RIGHT to ask for...

There are *so* many places we must exercise boundaries regularly: hair salon, in our homes, at the coffee bar/restaurant, while shopping, at the doctor's office/hospital, at work.

Recently, while on vacation, I went for a massage. My person asked if I had any requests, and I asked him specifically to do a *gentle sort of massage*, no deep pressure or anything like that. Ten minutes into the massage, he said, "I know you said you don't like deep tissue massage, but you're gonna thank me later for this, because you have a lot of knots in your back." And then he proceeded to give me a very deep tissue massage, which hurt a lot.

What did I do, you might ask? I wish I could report that: I immediately asked him to stop the massage, leapt off the table and left without tipping. Instead, I laid there in a curious state of mind, thinking, *maybe he's right. Maybe I will thank him*. Later, though, I just felt angry. And I tipped him too!

He totally trounced my simply stated boundary.

Unfortunately, even after we screw up enough courage to state our boundaries, the first thing that will often happen is that people will challenge the boundary. I wish it wasn't so. But it is.

Your boundaries are worth all the awkwardness and the repeating and the persistence.

**NEVER FORGET:** You have the right to ask for what you need/want, *and* you have the right to walk away from people, places, and situations when your boundaries are not being respected.

# Dear Magnificent Me,

Where have you put up a boundary, only to have the person **immediately disrespect** it. How did you handle it?

How does that inform what you need to do **now or next time**?

# Dear Great Mystery,

Please give me the courage to express my needs without apology.

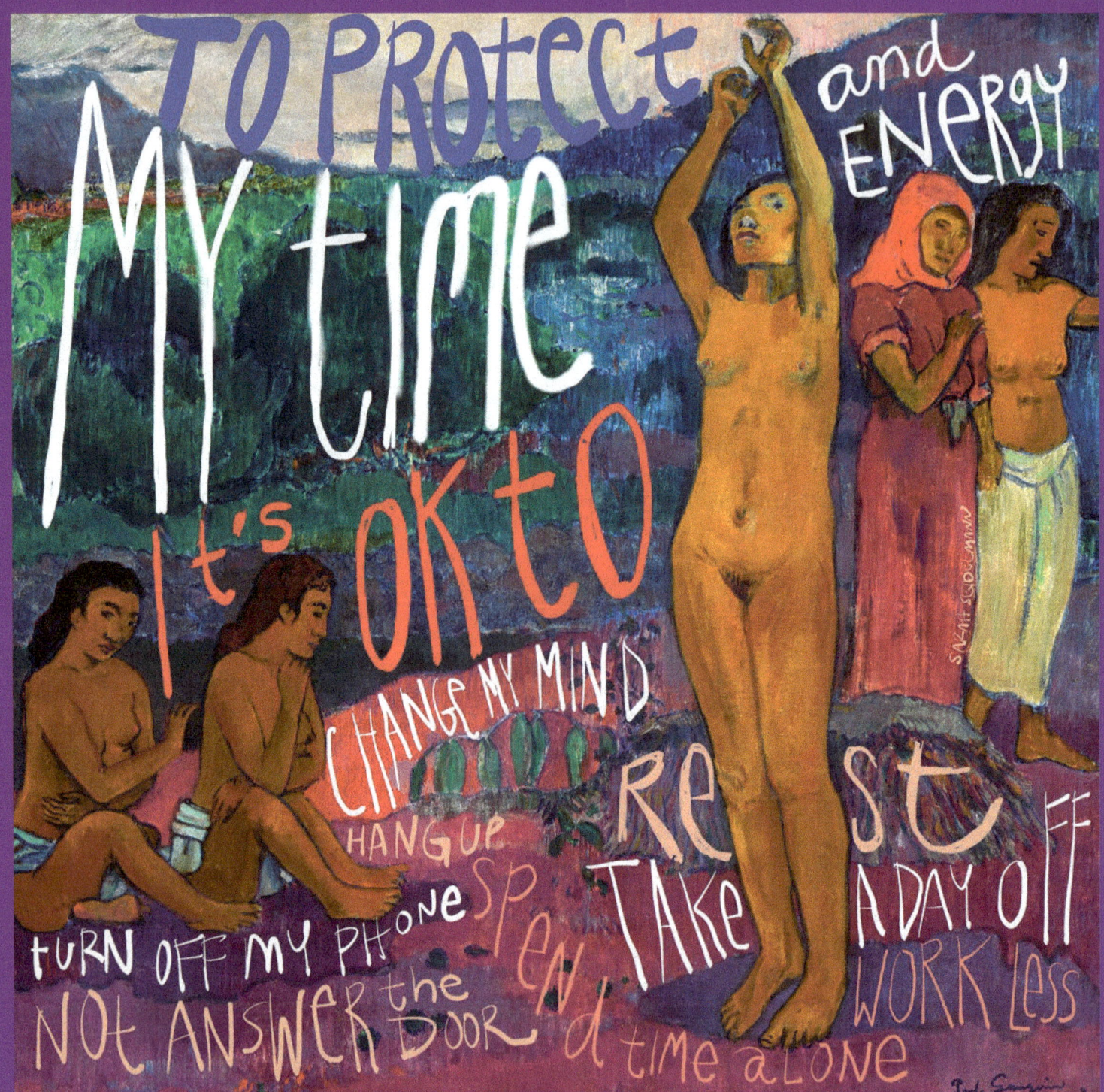

I struggle, in some moments, to make time for myself. Wow, even the compulsion to answer my phone immediately rather than let it go to voicemail when I don't have the bandwidth to respond can be hard! Taking an official day off with no real "assignment" can be so joyful for me, so why don't I do that more often?

Brené Brown speaks about how we hustle for our worthiness, and I think that's *exactly* what's underneath my own frequent inability to make space for me. If I'm working, I am worthy of love. My mom and dad worked tirelessly on many different projects throughout their lives and perhaps this is how my hustle became a thing? And I'm also truly passionate about my work and life, so choosing to step back sometimes requires discipline. I want to get better at leaving space, hitting pause, or napping.

 ## Dear Magnificent Me,

If you feel like you're not currently able to make space for yourself in your own life, why do you suppose that is?

What could you do today to step back from being a hustler and give yourself a moment of peace?

Complete these three sentences to see where you might have room to grow your own boundaries.

**❶** I have a right to ask for _____.
   (For example: More time to think about my decision, quiet uninterrupted time at home, or help with tasks at home or work.)

**❷** It is my right to protect my time/energy by choosing to _____.
   (For example: Take the day off, go on a sabbatical, or say no to an invitation for coffee with a lovely community member.)

**❸** I don't allow people to _____.
   (For example: Bully me into buying something, changing my mind, or altering my boundaries.)

# Dear Great Mystery,

Please show me where I need to speak up for myself, ask for what I need, and CLAIM MY SPACE.

INVADE my personal space, Ridicule me, tell racist jokes, Take people may not open my mail, their anger out on me, these things are not ok

SARAH SEIDELMANN

As this image says, "People may not invade my personal space, open my mail, take their anger out on me, or tell racist jokes around me. These things are not OK."

I had a conversation with my dad recently about boundaries with personal mail. For over fifty years of marriage, my mom would open occasionally open Dad's mail, even after he begged her not to. Neither of us truly understood why she continued to do that, but long after she died, the violation was still rehashed by my dad. He never found a way to successfully uphold that boundary with my mom. It led to unresolved feelings of anger.

So, when thinking about boundaries, it's also very important for me to think about where I might be, knowingly or unknowingly, violating the boundaries of others.

I just did it yesterday to one of my kids who asked me not to take a photo of them. *I did it anyway*, saying as I snapped the picture, "It's just for me. I won't show anyone." Sheesh. I apologized today, after becoming more fully conscious of what I'd done.

When somebody has violated a boundary of mine, I've often stayed silent, felt stunned and angry, and been unsure of what to say or do (at least in the moment).

What do you do when somebody **violates** a boundary of yours?

*No. 101*

# Dear Magnificent Me, (cont.)

What action could you take the **next time** your boundary is violated?

(For example: My dad could have gotten a post office box for himself. Inconvenient? Yes. But how far are we willing to go to protect our own boundaries? I suspect that him doing that could have preserved love in their relationship.)

# Dear Great Mystery,

Please make it clear to me in each moment what is not OK, so that I may TAKE AN ACTION TO PROTECT MYSELF and my boundaries.

*Action*

# Your Boundaries are a REFLECTION

> "Your boundaries are a reflection of how willing you are to advocate for the life that you want to create."
> —Nedra Tawwab, *Therapist*

If I have zero boundaries, I imagine my life is going to be a sort of aimless junk pile of responsibilities and activities. In that scenario, I am bitter, exhausted, and most probably not healthy in body, mind, or spirit.

With wonderful boundaries, and their influence of *intention*, my life can be a symphony of opportunities, rest, play, productive and meaningful work, and loving relationships.

Answer this question without editing yourself: *If my boundaries were an object what would they be?*

Do you like the metaphor you came up with? Or does it need some improvement?

When I answered that question, in my imagination I saw my boundaries as a huge horse pasture with rolling hills and a split-rail fence. As you might imagine, just about anything with two legs can find a way through that fence! My improvement would be to imagine my boundaries as an electric fence. Other beings would think long and hard before trying to get past an electric fence. And it would be plugged in 24/7!

# Dear Magnificent Me,

So, if your boundaries were an **object**, what would they be?

What would that metaphor look like in **real life**?

What **changes** might you need to make? For example: For me, if my boundaries are like an electric fence, I will have many fewer interlopers and my pasture will be more spacious! This means I need to take my boundaries deadly seriously...or else

# Dear Great Mystery,

Please teach me how to build a HOUSE OF BENEFICIAL BOUNDARIES so that I may thrive.

# DO NO HARM

AND TAKE ZERO BULLSHIT.

MOMMA ISN'T HAPPY

SARAH SEIDELMANN

# The BEASTIES
## have boundaries.

Doing this boundaries project feels so vulnerable. I can't control how others read into what I put on the images. That's the thing about art—you create it and then others take it in through their lens, and that's OK, and I have to remember that it's not about me.

Today I had no idea what I would create until I saw an adorable skunk waddle across the driveway during my walk today. Skunks are the ultimate boundary beastie—get too close and *BOOM*—*you will know* that you have overstepped a sacred threshold. Nothing personal!

The wild animals remind me that the boundaries of other beings are not *personal*, i.e., I don't need to take it like a knife to the heart if somebody doesn't want to talk with me or doesn't say yes to my invitation. The beasties naturally and spontaneously protect what they love (including themselves) and it's such a beautiful thing.

I have watched crows chase off predatory eagles, hummingbirds chase off other hungry hummingbirds, and territorial rhinos pee on certain dung heaps just to say, "HEY, THIS IS MY AREA. STAY AWAY."

I have felt like a momma bear in certain situations that pertained to my children, my BFF, or my momma when she was sick. A certain fierceness arises in me, and I will do whatever it takes to guard my beloved person, even if that means not being liked by somebody else.

HEY, THIS IS MY AREA STAY AWAY

The only person who can protect my time and space is ME.

*No. 107*

# Dear Magnificent Me,

Are you willing to **be fierce** on your own behalf, just like the beasties are?

# Dear Great Mystery,

Please help me to protect myself spontaneously and NATURALLY when necessary, so that I may truly live.

# THEY CAN'T kill you.

In the past, I got hurt by somebody very important to me. They kept stepping over my boundary again and again. I eventually realized that *it was me who provided them with the opportunity to hurt me in the first place*. I had never put up a boundary to begin with! Once I stopped sharing certain details of my life with them, the boundary was in place. They could no longer cause me pain.

I watched *Hustle* with Adam Sandler on Netflix this weekend (loved it!). In the film, a young basketball player is being bullied by another with verbal taunting. It's affecting his performance. The Adam character coaches his player to construct a boundary of sorts with the nasty person. Adam says to his player, "They can't kill you if you're already dead." In other words, "play dead" and don't react or give that bully any indication that his words bother you.

This is like the idea of *"gray-rocking"*, a technique I teach my clients if they are dealing with a person with some narcissist tendencies. If you're the target of a narcissist or bully, gray-rocking them is aiming to become extremely boring and unemotional, like a gray rock. You say very little and don't respond to their tirades or taunts with any emotion. Most bullies can't stand this. They want to get a reaction, and without one they will lose interest in you.

 **Dear Magnificent Me,**

Is there anybody in your life with whom being a **gray rock** might be beneficial?

 **Dear Great Mystery,**

Please teach me how to stay CALM and not react to those who might not have my best interests at heart.

# Boundaries Are ROOTS

If we want to grow a life that's like a magnificent mango tree, we must put down some deep roots (boundaries).

To make time for my art-making, for starters I have to put boundaries up with my other work (teaching or client coaching and healing work), my dogs (pugs can be persistent in their desire for more of *everything*!) and (sometimes) myself. Sometimes, "myself" would prefer to lie on the kitchen banquette sipping her third cup of decaf and scrolling through other artist websites than face the empty canvas. Deciding to block time on my calendar for art is a boundary that equals self-care, because my art is important to me. Saying no to an opportunity to do more "work" (i.e., work that is not making art) is a boundary. Choosing to thrift for clothes rather than buying new is another boundary with myself that allows me the freedom to splurge on paint and art books.

Dear Magnificent Me,

What roots (boundaries) are you putting down so that your life may grow into a great Mango tree and **bear juicy fruit**?

Dear Great Mystery,
Please help me tend myself with GREAT LOVE AND CARE
so that I might produce shade and sweet fruit for others to enjoy.

# Not Everybody WANTS a hug.

Physical boundaries are not something I think about often. I am a hugger by nature. However, I have had to put them up occasionally. I also remind myself that I need to honor others' physical boundaries. Not everybody wants a hug or a pat on the back.

Setting a physical boundary sounds like this:

> "Oh, actually I'm not much of a hugger, but I'd love to shake your paw!"

> "I'm not comfortable with making out here on the beach in front of everybody, but I'd love to smooch at home in private."

> "I've asked you not to touch me. Please stop now."

> "This journal is private. Please don't look at it ever again."

> "I don't want to sit on your lap. You are my professional colleague, and I would like to keep our relationship professional."

(That situation happened to me, but because the person was drunk, instead of saying anything, I simply moved away).

I don't...   I'm not...

*No. 115*

 # Dear Magnificent Me,

Are there any **physical boundaries** that you would like to set?

**What** do you need to say and **to whom**?

 # Dear Great Mystery,

Please remind me, when I need to be reminded, that I have a right to only be touched when I want to be touched and I have a right to ask for the kinds of touches that make me feel good.

# Boundaries Create SACRED
## space. sacred space. sacred space. sacred space.

I had a chance to be in a sweat lodge with dear friends recently and I made this art to remember the beauty. I realized that the sacred lodge cannot exist without boundaries. The lodge's "ribs" represent the ribs of Mother Earth. We crawl back into her womb to be cleansed by the fire + spirit, and we emerge reborn. None of this is possible without boundaries defining this sacred space.

It can be, scary to do your first lodge because it's so unknown and you must trust the person or people "pouring" the lodge. The first time I participated in one, I worried I wouldn't be able to handle the claustrophobia or the heat. Since then, I'm so grateful for all the lodges I have sat in and the profound healing and clarity that each one has brought me.

We need boundaries to create sacred space. These boundaries can look like the "ribs" of a lodge, or the formal intention or agreement of a group to listen and not interrupt. There are many ways to

create sacred space **together.**

# Dear Magnificent Me,

When you create sacred space for yourself or others, what **tools or agreements** create those boundaries?

# Dear Great Mystery,

Please help me remember that I know how to use boundaries to create SACRED SPACE and remind me how to do it if I forget.

# DOORS CAN CREATE BOUNDARIES
### opened or closed.

The home as a metaphor for boundaries has been powerful for me. In our house, there are five of us living here, and doors provide a way to create a boundary when we each need quietude or to be alone.

I shut the door to my little home office when I pray or take a shamanic journey or, sometimes, when I need to cry and sit with myself.

My open door, in contrast, says

"I'm open to interruptions and visitors."

When I used to work at the hospital, my door (and the notes I posted on it!) was my main boundary tool.

One day I was pumping breast milk (I had two horns attached to my breasts and the milking machinery was running) and had posted a sign on the door:

**DO NOT ENTER!!**

One of the gastroenterologists came barreling in and began rattling off his patient's clinical details to me and it took him a minute before he finally looked up and saw me with my breasts hanging out.

He skedaddled quickly.

*No. 121*

# Dear Magnificent Me,

Do you use **doors** as boundaries effectively?

If not, **what** would you like to try?

# Dear Great Mystery,

Please remind me that creating a boundary can be as simple as closing (or locking) a door for a period. Help me have the courage to take the time I need for myself.

# HAELLL NO!

We all know which things feel like a *hell no*, but do we always honor that knowing?

Some examples of hell no's:

"Do you want to come over and have some fun in the bedroom?" HAELLL NO

(From your remarried ex-husband)

"Can you give up a week of your paid vacation for a work 'retreat'?" HAELLL NO

"Would you like to pet my black mamba snake?" HAELLL NO

"Is it cool if I pack lutefisk for your lunch?" HAELLL NO

"Can you watch our four kids and two pit bulls for two weeks?" HAELLL NO

Saying no flies in the face of what so many of us were taught as children. Many of us still struggle just to get this word out. *It is OK to say no.* And the more we do it, the easier it gets. I can't believe how many times I have said no this year—and the creative and kind ways I have found to do it!

# Dear Magnificent Me,

When was the last time you felt a huge NO swell up inside you and then proceeded to **ignore** that voice and acquiesce?

How could you **prevent** such an occurrence in the future?

# Dear Great Mystery,

Please help me to **hear** that sacred inner NO loud and clear when it rises within me so that I can **OBEY** it.

*No. 125*

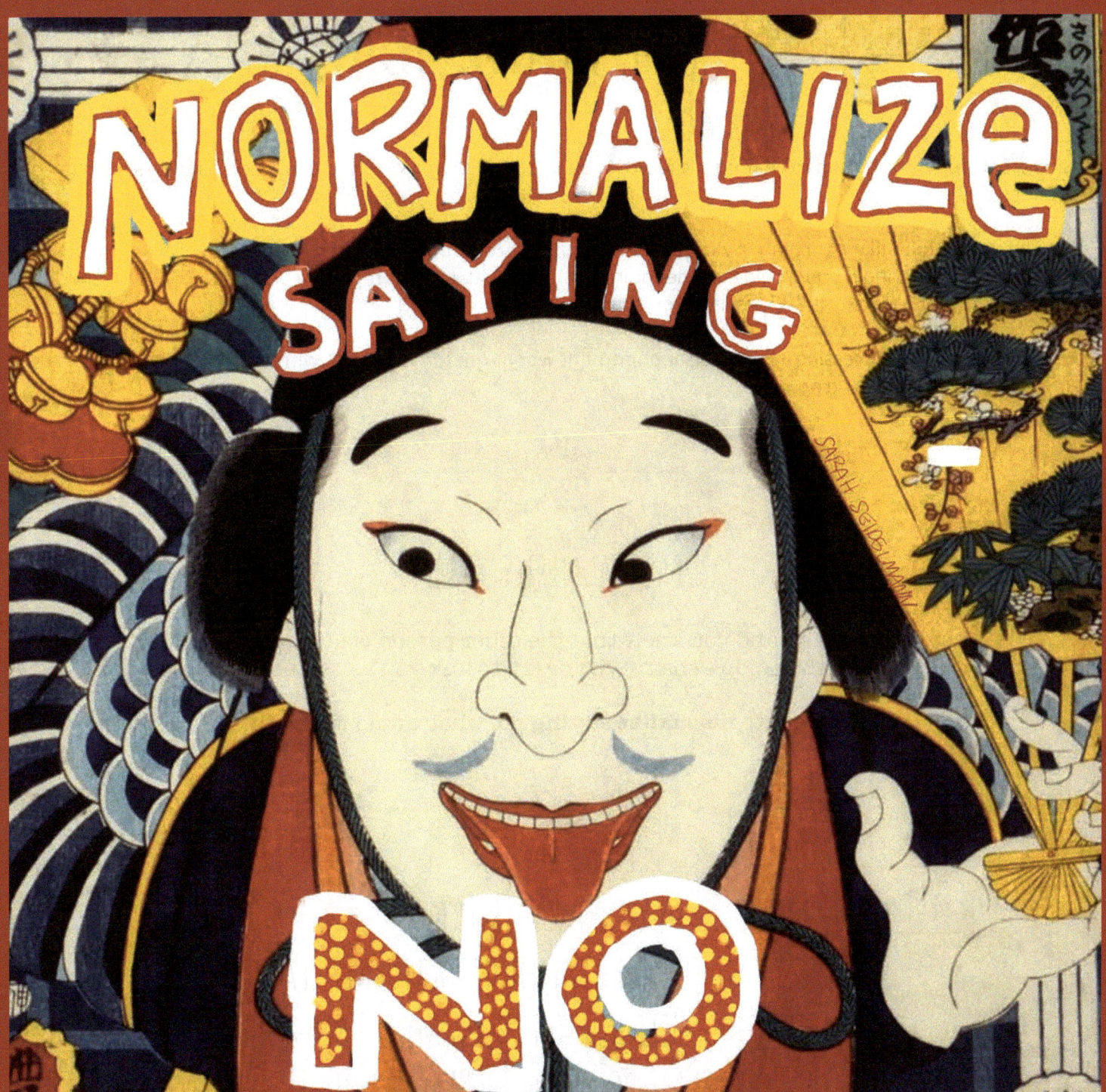

# Normalize Saying NO

What if we were *all* more used to hearing the word no and being OK with it? What would normalizing saying no look like in society?

For me, it would look like couching my requests with an obvious option for them to turn me down. "Hello, dear [person]. I am wondering if you would consider doing [activity] with me. I completely understand if your schedule is too busy to accommodate this. I appreciate you so much, no matter what!"

It would also look like processing my own disappointment when I get turned down, without making the other person feel shame or guilt for saying no.

### Dear Magnificent Me,

When have you said no and you knew that the other person was **completely OK** with it (i.e., they didn't shame you or try to talk you into it, etc.)?

If you were to **normalize saying no**, what would it look like?

### Dear Great Mystery,
Please help me to make saying no a normal part of EVERY SINGLE DAY. Help me to process my feelings when others turn me down and I'm disappointed.

# ASK PERMISSION

To promote good boundaries in our relationships it's good to make a practice of asking permission.

## This is boundary activism!

In my most intimate relationships, I often forget to ask permission.

We can ask permission about little things, like I can ask my partner,

> "How do you feel about me adding curry to this soup I'm making for dinner?"

That's a kind thing to do in case I'm the only one of us in a mood for something spicy and curried. I can easily curry up just one of our bowls!

And we can ask permission about bigger things, like I can ask my highly sensitive child,

> "I know you're trying to get homework done. Would it be OK if I vacuum right now?"

(Confession: I've never done this in real life, but I aim to become the person who is capable of this!)

Anne Lamott teases that "If people wanted you to write warmly about them better, they should have behaved better," but I imagine that she probably checks in with at least *some* of her beloveds before sharing parts of their stories. I know that I have done that type of boundary-checking.

This is the golden rule of boundaries:

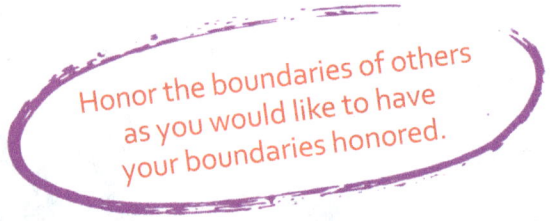

Honor the boundaries of others as you would like to have your boundaries honored.

# Dear Magnificent Me,

Is there some place in your relationships it might be good for you to do **more asking for permission**?

# Dear Great Mystery,

Please remind me gently when it would be best for me to ask permission BEFORE proceeding. Help me to act with respect for the boundaries of others.

# Staying Out of God's business.

Sometimes, for me, having boundaries is about recognizing what is mine to carry and what is the Great Mystery's to carry.

My dad (age 82) was feeling suicidal again today *and* I have COVID *and* I am reminded of how hard it is for me to surrender when my loved ones are suffering. My dad's deep psychic pain belongs to him, but I can very easily take it on as my own—and suffer more than is necessary.

Many troubles in this life (like Dad's suicidal ideation, babies who are sick in the ICU, war...) are way above my pay grade. I can't shoulder that kind of responsibility, but I can surrender my dad (and his pain) to God. And I can bear witness to his suffering. I can be present with him.*

*Update: My dad turned the corner in the fall and stopped feeling suicidal. He died six months prior to the publishing of this book and is now fully free from suffering. I miss him so much.

# Dear Magnificent Me,

Do you **struggle** when your beloveds are suffering or in distress? What would surrender look like for you?

Do you know the **Serenity Prayer**? I said the Serenity Prayer (below) a bunch yesterday and twice today. It really is the best damn boundary prayer there is.

God grant me the serenity to accept the things I cannot change, the courage to change the things I can, and the WISDOM to know the difference.

# It's Okay to take the day OFF

Today I was realizing how hard it is for me (*still!*) to accept that when I'm sick, I need to ask for help, cancel work, get a sub. I think I learned this horrible pattern, ironically, when I practiced the healing art of allopathic medicine. *We were all always expected to "man-up" and show up*. Or, at least, it felt that way to me.

Today, sick as a dog with COVID, I had to engage in two-way prayer. It's a practice where you write to God/the Universe and ask for help, and God answers when you write back to yourself. As God, you write with your non-dominant hand. When I did this today, I got the memo (from God, no less) that *I truly needed to call in sick for my teaching job*. Thank goodness I did, as yesterday ended up being a long, awful fever dream of a day and I felt progressively sicker and sicker.

## Dear Magnificent Me,

When you are sick or, for whatever reason, you sense it would be best to tend to yourself, **how easy** is it for you to ask for what you need?

Is there somebody you admire who does an excellent job of taking care of themselves regarding work? Would you be willing to you **ask them** how they ask for what they need and try out some of their techniques?

## Dear Great Mystery,
## Please help me to remember that nothing is more important than tending to my own well-being.

*No. 135*

MEDITATION MELTS the BOUNDARY BETWEEN ME AND the UNIVERSE.

SARAH SEDLMANN

# Some Boundaries are best DISSOLVED

I have noticed that some boundaries are meant to dissolved. Like the boundary between me and God/the Universe, for example. One of the ways I can dissolve this perceived boundary is by meditating or spending time out in the woods alone in silence. When I feel separate from this benevolence, I'm bound to suffer. Those simple practices allow me to sense the pure peace and absolute stillness that the Universe is always vibrating. Here with the Universe, I know it's all going to be OK.

This perceived wall between myself and the Great Mystery happens whenever a wounded part of me takes over. Maybe I get triggered by something someone does or says and a part of me who is definitely *not* Godlike takes over. But this is the one boundary I must always take care to dissolve, so that I can recharge my battery and receive wisdom from the Great Mystery.

### Dear Magnificent Me,

How do you dissolve the boundary between you and God/the Universe **most easily**?

When was the last time you remember **consciously doing it** and how did it feel?

### Dear Great Mystery,
Please help me to find simple ways to connect with you and to feel your presence and peace so that I may RADIATE that sensation into the cosmos.

# Teach the CHILDREN well.

When I think of all the ways we teach our children to comply and be "nice," I shudder. In some instances, I get righteously ticked off. I've done my best to teach my kids to have empowered boundaries, and I think I've done OK.

Wouldn't it be amazing if we taught boundaries at home and in school from an early age and we respected our own children's boundaries?

Could it be OK for kids to say to Uncle Roger or Aunt Linda, "No, thank you. I don't want a hug from you." Or to say to a parent, "I know Grandma and Grandpa are coming to visit, but I get really bored when you guys talk for hours, so I'm going to go upstairs and play with my LEGO instead."

> It sure is complicated business, but teaching children to be sovereign beings and training them, through our own actions, *that it is absolutely OK and necessary to say no,* is important work.

# Dear Magnificent Me,

What do you wish your **parents** would have taught you differently about boundaries?

# Dear Great Mystery,

when I can guide children, Please may I demonstrate the use of HEALTHY boundaries and support them in stating their own needs.

# Boundaries can be places of CONFLICT

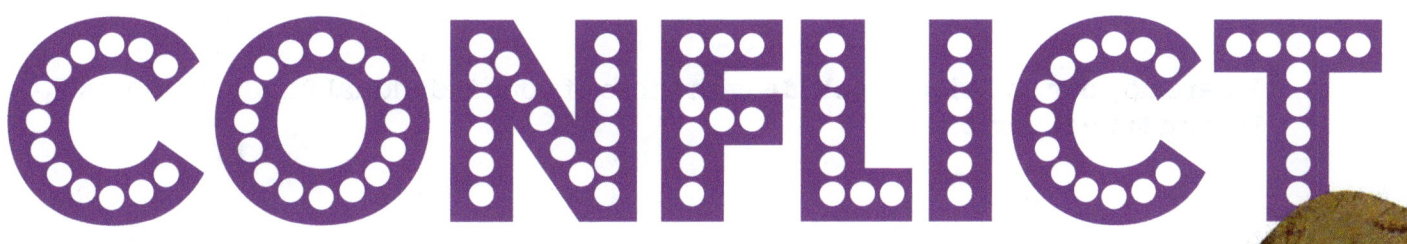

This is a message I received from my Core Beastie (spirit animal), Alice the Elephant, that inspired the art to the left:

 "Boundaries in a family can be delicate things. On one hand, you crave being a unit, all together. But your soul will require you to carve out your own specific space. All those individual spaces can overlap, and that's where conflict can arise."

Sometimes I can feel "needy," like I want to hang with somebody in my chosen family ("Let's go thrifting! Or for a walk on the lake! Or can we go to the movies tonight?"). My desire, however, doesn't always intersect with my beloveds' idea of a good time. They may be craving alone time or want to go out with friends instead.

Physical boundaries come up often when we live together. Maybe I was counting on doing yoga in the family room and Charlie wants to have friends hang in that same space. Navigating these boundaries requires compassion, flexibility, and good communication. For example, I can say to Charlie, "I was hoping to do yoga in this space now. Would you be willing to tell your friends to come over in thirty minutes? I won't take long."

My work is to not take my family members' boundaries personally. They are simply taking care of themselves.

And I need to find a way to do that too.

# Dear Magnificent Me,

Where do your boundaries **collide** with those of your individual family members'? **Do you take it personally?**

How would you like to handle these differences in the **future**?

# Dear Great Mystery,

Please help me to breathe and remember that we all have boundaries that we need to UPHOLD and it is not personal.

# Boundaries create our IDENTITY

Self-boundaries are perhaps the *most* challenging of all for me. Using the phrase "I don't"—instead of "I can't" or "I shouldn't"—helps me be in integrity with the identity I choose to inhabit.

I **don't** eat sugar or flour.

I **don't** respond to text messages from strangers.

I **don't** argue with strangers on the Internet.

I **don't** shop impulsively.

I **don't** gossip.

I want to *be* the kind of person who doesn't do any of the things above.

Am I perfect at this? Heck no! The odd, ridiculous Anthropology purchase happens! And I have had to call and apologize when I spilled beans that I shouldn't have when I gossiped. I have gone into the ditch with eating flour and sugar.

But when I speak my intention out loud, do I feel stronger?

Do I feel more amazing each moment that I adhere to my own set of inner laws?

Yes! Yes!

THIS IS THE PERSON I AM BECOMING

*No. 145*

# Dear Magnificent Me,

What is the **identity** you want to embrace?

What is on that **identity's** "I don't _____" list?

# Dear Great Mystery,

Please help me to stay in integrity with myself so that I may operate on the HIGHEST plane possible for me.

# DON'T ANSWER it.

My phone has been by my side nearly continuously for the last 26 years (especially during the school days when one of my kids might need me).

Let's begin the phone boundaries convo with the simple occurrence of a phone ringing. I used to have an irresistible urge to answer my phone, *even when I knew exactly who was calling and I knew I did not have the bandwidth to speak with them.*

I could feel my hand raise the phone to my ear and the internal shout arising in my chest of *Nooooooo....!* and then suddenly I'd be chatting in a sing-songy voice and simultaneously be feeling weirdly dead inside. I wasn't doing anybody any favors, especially the person who called me.

These days, I have no problem letting calls go to voicemail. I have a rule: If I don't know who is calling, I do not under any circumstances pick up. POTUS or Deepak Chopra can leave a message!

**I dream of a world where everybody puts their phones away when we go out for dinner… and we deeply listen to each other.**

# Dear Magnificent Me,

Where do you wish you had a **better boundary with your phone**?

How could you **practice** this? (For example: For a period, I kept my phone in the bathroom at night instead of next to my bed. It was heaven. Once we had teenagers, I wasn't willing to do that anymore.)

# Dear Great Mystery,

Please help me to keep the phone (and all of its pinging and ringing) in the right place in my life. Help me to BE PRESENT for my **LIFE** and for the **HUMANS** and **OTHER BEINGS** in it.

*No. 149*

"Building a connection to yourself and trusting that connection is the foundation of boundaries."
— Sarri Gilman

I see you and I will care for you no matter what.

@sarahseidelmann

TRANSFORMING YOUR BOUNDARIES

# SELF Connection
## is the foundation of boundaries.

In therapist Sarri Gilmans's book *Transforming Your Boundaries*, she introduces the idea that without a strong connection to self, *boundaries aren't going to happen.*

Let's drill down into this idea. We only tenderly care for those who we love. If our boundaries aren't strong, we can assume that we need to connect with ourselves more. We can begin to heal by taking gentle care of ourselves, by listening to our needs and our inner voice. Caring for ourselves signals to us that we are worth caring for, that we can and should have boundaries to protect and honor our needs and wants.

### Dear Magnificent Me,

When or with whom have you had **insufficient boundaries** to the point that you became exhausted, irritated, or resentful?

How did you feel **toward yourself** during that time? How did you treat yourself?

What action could you take today to **show yourself that you matter**?

### Dear Great Mystery,
Please help me to foster a deep and LOVING CONNECTION
**TO MYSELF** so that I may be more effective in my life.

# CO-DEPENDENCY VENN DIAGRAM

*Don't do for others what they are capable of doing for themselves!*

- **Doing things for other people**
- **Helping**
- **Enabling**
- **Things people cannot do for themselves**
- **Things people are able (and should) to do for themselves.**

SARAH SEIDELMANN

# SOMETIMES a boundary means standing DOWN

This diagram was inspired by another meme and reminds me of an everlasting truth I learned during a two-year period of being in a twelve-step group for co-dependents (Al-anon): **Don't do anything for a person that they can (and should) do for themselves.**

That seems so simple. However, it was not clear to me for a long time. Maybe because we had addiction in our family (my paternal grandmother). Or maybe I struggled with this boundary because I am a highly sensitive person (HSP). Or both. All I know is that I'm not alone.

I talk to people weekly who are so disturbed by the suffering of another person in their life that they attempt to save that person from certain failure or negative con-sequences. They are doing things that the other person can and should be doing for themselves. Things like paying their bills, doing their laundry, taking care of their dog, repairing their vehicle, taking care of their kids, etc.

I've been guilty of this too. What I know from my own experience is that continuing to have no boundaries by doing things for another person *that they can and should be doing themselves* results in becoming resentful.

But there's GOOD NEWS!

You can learn to stop this pattern, and that will preserve the **love that exists.**

# Dear Magnificent Me,

Are you doing anything for an adolescent or adult these days that they **should and could be doing for themselves but aren't** (maybe because of their drinking, overspending, overeating, or gambling, or for some other reason)?

If so, would you like to **stop**? (I suggest Al-Anon as a starting point, even if alcohol isn't a factor. It's free!)

# Dear Great Mystery,

Please show me when and if I should be helping another person. Let me know when it would be **best** for me to let someone I love experience the natural consequences of their actions.

# YOU MIGHT need to create a SERVICE

Sometimes creating a boundary can be done by creating a new offering.

That's what I did. I created a Pick My Brain session option on my website, which enabled me to offer space to folks looking to ask me for professional advice or consultation—for example, when somebody contacts me and wants professional guidance, wants to learn how to write/publish books, or whatever else they might want to know. That was hard, at first, as I worried that people would think I wasn't "nice" because I wasn't willing to give my time and share what I've learned for free, without limits.

For years I have offered support in many different forms for free—weekly writing, YouTube videos, serving on non-profit boards, volunteering, and hundreds of podcast interviews—and I still do.

However, I now prioritize my own creative and personal time outside of work, and so having this Pick My Brain service has been the perfect boundary for me at work.

### Pick my Brain!

On totems, coaching, shamanism, healing, writing...life!
OR very focused coaching session for an existing client.

Book Now >

*No. 156*

# Dear Magnificent Me,

Do you run a business and **need a Pick My Brain service**? Or do you even want others to pick your brain?

Where do you need to put up a boundary **at home or work**?

How could you create a policy or other creative possibility that would make that boundary **easier to uphold**?

# Dear Great Mystery,

Please help me to trust that it's OK to get paid for what I have learned, and it's OK to choose when and how I gift my service to others.

*No. 157*

# THERE IS SAFETY WITHIN

*family.*

As I continued to explore boundaries, I asked Alice the elephant—my spirit animal Core Beastie*—to offer me a teaching I could share about boundaries. She always offers a fresh perspective. Here's what she told me:

> "There is safety and calm within the boundaries of a family. This is a boundary that is very sacred. Elephants know how to protect their family from those who wish to disrupt that space. Families need to shore up that boundary so they can spend uninterrupted time together. We do that by playing and resting together in stillness."
> –Alice

I realize that not all families feel safe to be in. So, rather, let's think of our *chosen families*. Whether it's the family you grew up in or one you assembled from scratch with the people (or person) you love most in the world, it is precious and can be an island of safety.

I myself have been an "interloper" who has made others in my own family feel unsafe by offering my unsolicited advice or by sharing my anxious concerns with them about their life or life choices. Gah! I am working on it!

When I think of activities that shore up our family, I think of: quiet fires in the living room fireplace with music playing and books being read, long walks in the woods with my daughter or my husband, fun outings at thrift shops with a common goal in mind, and working on a larger creative project together.

When I think of having strong boundaries around my family, I get a little anxious because i*ncluding others is so important to me*. My family was formed, in part, through the bonds of adoption, so I bristle a little when people talk about "blood family." For me, it is a *choice* to be family. A family bond is special, and we can extend that specialness to others outside of our chosen family too.

*Curious about who your Core Beastie might be? Take a guided shamanic journey, as my treat to you! Go to: followyourfeelgood.com/discover-your-core-beastie

 ## Dear Magnificent Me,

Does your special family have a way of **shoring up your boundaries together**?

If not, would you like to try it? **What would that look like?**

 ## Dear Great Mystery,

Please help me to honor the beautiful, **sacred family** that you have given me and help me to nurture it.

# OMG no!

Over twenty years ago, my husband and I rented a sixteen-foot truck, the largest we'd used yet, to hold all of our worldly possessions. My parents came to help us load the truck. After the twentieth trip to the moving truck with a box, my mom looked me dead in the eye and said, "Honey, this is the last time we can help you move." After I got over being mildly offended (I was 27 years old and still believed the moon and sun set around *me*), I completely understood. I think that was also the move when my husband had us load a cord of firewood along with everything else!

It is OK to be exhausted.

It is OK to say no.

It is OK to say no. It's OK to say no. It's OK to say no. It's OK to say no. It's OK to say no.

It's OK.

Saying yes when our brain is screaming

## "HELL NO!"

will only lead to resentment and heartache.

If you want to preserve your sanity, and the friendship or relationship, it's best to decline if you're not into it.

# Dear Magnificent Me,

When was the most recent time that you said yes (while smiling) and **your brain shouted NO! WTF!?**

How could you have **declined kindly and honestly?** What might you have offered instead (if anything)? (For example: "I can watch your dogs while you move." Or "I'd be happy to show up with a bucket of chicken and bottles of Hawaiian Punch when the last truck is empty.")

# Dear Great Mystery,

Please help me to become more aware of my inner compass that says YES AND NO so that I can prevent future resentments.

*No. 163*

"I really need you!"

"What would it look like to NOT betray myself?"

SARAH SEIDELMANN

# Boundaries keep us from BETRAYING ourselves.

I had a wonderful convo with my coaching colleague Dipa about boundaries. Here's what Dipa shared: "To me, boundaries are the opposite of self-betrayal. Whenever I am unsure about my boundaries, I ask myself, *what would I do in this situation if I didn't betray myself?* This helps me so much. When I betray myself, I automatically end up betraying others too. If I do not also put myself within my own circle of compassion along with the others, I am betraying myself. It's sort of like having equal rights to my own compassion."

Dipa's words resonated so much for me. Why am I so willing to throw myself under the bus at times? I believe our culture has shamed us into believing that self-sacrifice is always honorable.

We will always be needed, hopefully. Our kids need us. Our partner needs us. Our BFF needs us. Our colleagues too. But to even begin to show up for others, *we need to be loyal to ourselves first and last.*

None of us wants to be betrayed—least of all by ourselves! Boundaries are the only way to prevent it.

### Dear Magnificent Me,

When was the last time **you betrayed yourself in some way**, large or small? Why did you do it?

What would it have looked like to **remain loyal to yourself**, to your soul?

### Dear Great Mystery,
Please help me to stay compassionate and caring with myself. Keep me from betraying myself, so that I may be of true service when the time is right

# boundary... NOT ULTIMATUM

I haven't used boundaries very often as ultimatums (except when parenting), but when I have it has felt extremely important. There are subtle differences between boundaries and ultimatums. Sophie Gray explains the difference:

> Generally speaking, ultimatums are about force: usually involving a threat or demand that attempts to control another person. Boundaries, however, are about personal power: a limit that you set for yourself, around yourself, that does not come from a place of anger, judgement, or blame.
>
> In theory, there's a difference, but how does that play out in practice?
>
> For example: "We are done if you ever speak to them again" versus "I am really uncomfortable with you talking to this person, and I don't think I can continue the relationship if that continues"
>
> —Therapist Sophie Gray (of thinkgray.com)

Try it out. Clearly outline the consequence for violating a boundary. Let's say your boundary relates to body and weight-related talk with your family. You can say something like, "Mom, I feel uncomfortable when you constantly talk about who is fat or thin around the kids. And please refrain from commenting on my kids' physical appearance or weight. If this is not something you can agree to, we will have to leave early to take you back home."

Melissa Urban writes, in her book *The Book of Boundaries: End Resentment, Burnout, and Anxiety—and Reclaim Your Time, Energy, Health, and Relationships* that,

> A boundary doesn't tell someone else what to do, **it tells them what you will do."**

*No. 167*

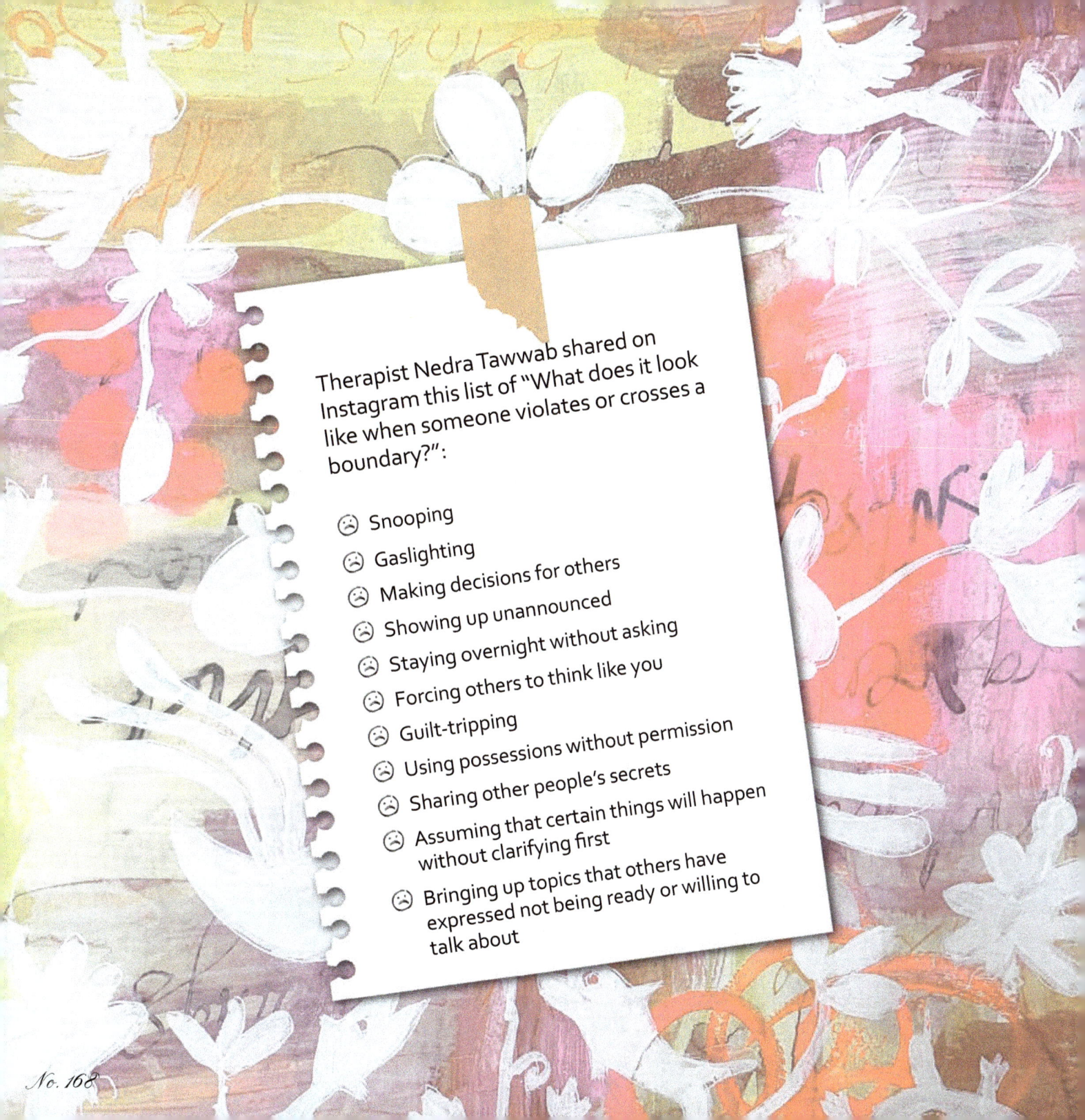

Therapist Nedra Tawwab shared on Instagram this list of "What does it look like when someone violates or crosses a boundary?":

- ☹ Snooping
- ☹ Gaslighting
- ☹ Making decisions for others
- ☹ Showing up unannounced
- ☹ Staying overnight without asking
- ☹ Forcing others to think like you
- ☹ Guilt-tripping
- ☹ Using possessions without permission
- ☹ Sharing other people's secrets
- ☹ Assuming that certain things will happen without clarifying first
- ☹ Bringing up topics that others have expressed not being ready or willing to talk about

# Dear Magnificent Me,

Have you ever put up a boundary and **stated what action you would take** if your boundary was violated? How did it go?

Would you like to try setting a **boundary with a consequence now** somewhere in your life? (For example: "If you do [action that ignores your boundary] again, then I will [action you will take in response].")

# Dear Great Mystery,

Please help me to clearly communicate my boundaries with others, including, when necessary, what actions I will take if my boundaries are violated.

you will encounter pushback.  98% GUARANTEED

My courageous and clear boundaries are not always met with joy. It can be challenging to co-exist with each other. But we are not responsible for the reactions of others. We must continue to ask for what we need. If our boundary is not respected, then we can make a different choice.

We have a huge open shelf in our back hall that was endlessly filled with stuff—bowls, Crockpots, things on their way to the basement, recycling, old jars. That kind of clutter overwhelms my ADHD brain and, one day, I gently explained to my partner Mark (OK, maybe not *gently*. I may have been quite animated) that I needed that space to remain clear. Mark was not super enthusiastic, but he agreed. Two weeks later, he brashly placed an empty plastic jug there on my *keep-it-clear* shelf. When I reminded him of the new clear-shelf policy he said, "Geez. This jug is just on its way to the recycling. Where else am I supposed to put it?" I repeated my desperate need for reduction in visual clutter and he agreed to clear the jug. There has only been one more incident and otherwise that shelf has been gloriously *clear* since then!

What's important to *us* may not be important to our beloveds (or colleagues or roommates), but we can still ask for what we need. It may take two, three, or ten reminders to solidify your new boundary with others. Don't give up!

## Dear Magnificent Me,

When was the last time you set a boundary and got some **flack or pushback** for it? How could you deal with the discomfort of sitting with other people's reactions to your boundaries?

## Dear Great Mystery,
Please help me stay rooted in my convictions when I am setting healthy boundaries, so that I may weather any storm.

"When we learn to say no, we stop lying."

— Melody Beattie

# SAYING YES when we mean no is a LIE

Melanie Beattie said, "When we learn to say no, we stop lying." A dear friend shared this quote with me. Does it get any straighter than that? It feels *sooooo* right.

**Creating and maintaining boundaries is really about honesty and living in our own truth.**

I have said yes when I meant no so many times in my life. It feels horrible. Why? Because *lying* feels horrible. I was out of integrity in that moment, and my body knew it.

When you're deciding whether to say yes or no to a request and you find yourself thinking, *I should say yes,* it's likely that your inner people-pleaser has taken the wheel. If you don't check yourself, you're going to be baking banana bread for the PTA sale with a sense of bitterness right quick.

My inner people-pleaser is just trying to keep me safe (I want to belong!) and has *no problem* with lying about banana bread for the PTA. But I have to live in this body and face myself, so I (my higher self) have to step in and be honest. If being honest will harm someone, I will pray for a way to stay in my truth without harming others, whenever possible.

## Dear Magnificent Me,

When was the last time you lied and said yes instead of being honest and saying no? **How did lying feel**? How could you do it differently next time?

## Dear Great Mystery,

Please help me to BE HONEST, except when to do so would harm another person. In those situations, please give me guidance so that I might live in my integrity.

# BUILD  A BOUNDARY sandwich.

Boundary-setting is often hard simply because we may have very few boundary skills. We need to share our diverse scripts, ideas, and creative methods of saying no with each other and our kids, colleagues, and partners. Let's get better together!

A fun boundary skill to try is to build a boundary sandwich. This idea for this image came from somebody talking about criticism and how to offer it. Stating a boundary is, in a way, akin to offering a critique, because we are bound to get a response and the response is likely to be (or at least may be) negative.

*Nobody wants to hear the word no,* and nobody wants to be criticized.

To be clear, though: When we put up a boundary, we are not criticizing anybody. We are simply stating what we are willing or not willing to do/be/endure.

Clamping a boundary between positives to make a sandwich can soften the information. It might look like this:

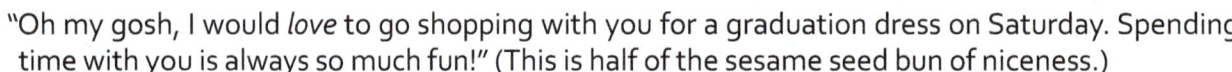

"Oh my gosh, I would *love* to go shopping with you for a graduation dress on Saturday. Spending time with you is always so much fun!" (This is half of the sesame seed bun of niceness.)

"*This* Saturday, however, I committed to myself that I would work on writing my boundaries book from 9 a.m. until 2 p.m., so I can't leave until then." (This is the boundary-holding hard part, as the request from my daughter was to go dress shopping at 10 a.m.).

"I'm so glad you asked me! I hope we can still go at 2 p.m., if that works for you, but I totally understand if you want to ask somebody else." (The other half of the sesame seed bun of niceness.)

Another example:

 Thank you *so much* for thinking of me for the 2024 *Balling Shamanic Babes* event. Everything you create is so amazing! This spring, however, I am committed to painting my face off, and to do that I need to paint on Saturdays too. Even though I can't do it this year, I would love to donate a set of my books to the event, if you'd like."

# Dear Magnificent Me,

Have you ever used the **sandwich technique for boundaries**? If so, how did it go?

Who do you know who is an **ace at setting boundaries**? Could you **ask them** for a few of their best lines and write them down for future use?

# Dear Great Mystery,

Please give me the gentle words or CREATIVE PROSE to say no in a KIND AND CONSTRUCTIVE WAY.

asking for what you need

# ISN'T BEING EXTRA

Let's look at the topic of hearing the words, "Sorry. Is that okay?" when you're in a service situation of some kind. This sort of boundary issue comes up most often for me when I am out of my element and at a restaurant, salon, or in some other situation where I am being served or waited upon.

Reminder: It is always OK to ask for exactly what you want. *You are the customer*.

If you are in the service industry yourself, you may have no problem asking for exactly what you want or turning down whatever less-than-acceptable alternative you have been offered. I'm not always super comfortable with it.

Sarah Knight, the author of *F*ck No!* explains:

Let's say you're at a restaurant and because you are a responsible customer who doesn't assume a kitchen can just provide whatever you happen to be in the mood for that day, you read the menu. Good work. You settle on your order—again, straight off the menu—but a few details remain unclear. For example, the menu says "cola" or "mustard" but doesn't specify which kind of each. So when you relay your order to the waiter, you say exactly what you want—Diet Coke and Dijon.

At which point the waiter tells you they serve only Pepsi products and yellow mustard: "Sorry, is that okay?"

If you can't, shouldn't, or don't want to accept the substitute, then *you do not have to say yes*.

It isn't being EXTRA to state your requests or to pay for exoskeleton polishing services *only* when they are delivered by the one and only Bruce, whom you absolutely adore!

# Dear Magnificent Me,

Have you recently had the opportunity to **clearly say no to a service** (or a beverage or food item) that was not what you wanted or asked for? If you didn't say no, what stopped you?

# Dear Great Mystery,

Please remind me that I'm not being EXTRA when I ask for what I need or make a request to have something corrected on my behalf.

Setting boundaries is not mean. We can set them with Love in our hearts. We must be willing to be UNCOMFORtable.

— Sarah Seidelmann

# THIS is UNCOMFORTABLE!

This common belief that boundaries are somehow mean or unloving is just f*cking hogwash and must be banished. What *is* true is that putting up boundaries can feel very uncomfortable at first.

A few summers after my mom died, my dad started coming over to our house unannounced and hanging out in the living room. It unnerved our kids at different points (being teenagers, they felt their space was invaded), and sometimes it rocked my world (because if my dad showed up, I felt like I couldn't continue on with my own creative work or whatever I had scheduled).

Finally, after agonizing over it, I spoke to Dad about it. I let him know that we loved having him over, *but that we needed a heads-up—a text or a phone call.* That hurt my dad's feelings. *I felt terrible.* However, it was something that we needed to address for everybody's space to feel respected.

*This is not comfortable work.*

### Dear Magnificent Me,

As you read that story, did a particular boundary issue **pop up** for you?

What was it and **what step might you take next**?

### Dear Great Mystery,
### Please help me to get through even the most uncomfortable situations in order to be clear about my needs.

# BOUNDARY-Crasher

thats me!

My boundaries are a work in progress, far from perfect. A case in point: As our food was delivered by our waitress last night, I instinctively reached across the table to test a bit of one of my daughters' dinners without asking. Gah! Immediately, the chorus rang out from both daughters. *"Mom! Boundaries!"* I tend to ignore this particular boundary of politeness and personal food sovereignty. I'm working on it.

Other ways I have recently been a boundary crasher: Unsolicited, I went on GlassDoor.com and suggested several different jobs for my adult daughter after she said she was applying for summer jobs. (Boundary: She's 21 years old and can find her own jobs without my help.)

I talked over my 18-year-old *during their doctor's appointment*, thinking I really needed to tell the doctor a few important things. (Boundary: I can sit and be quiet and just be a support unless I am asked to speak.)

I suggested to my husband something about his career path. (Boundary: The man is 57 years old and has never needed my vocational dictatorship.)

## Dear Magnificent Me,

Have you been **busted** for having bad boundaries?

When, where, and with whom are you most likely to **trounce** all over somebody's boundaries?

## Dear Great Mystery,
Please help me keep my sticky fingers off other people's plates and out of their business! Thank you.

*No. 183*

# nice-girl/boy Non-Binary SYNDROME

My co-dependent tendencies popped up this weekend with my dear dad. I got in a real snafu because he was suffering, and I believed I had to fix him. In these dark times, I feel like I'll never learn. So I gave myself permission to be human—for the 43,9000th time. I need self-compassion too, if I'm ever going to get better with this stuff.

Beverly Engel wrote, in *The Nice Girl Syndrome:*

> " Stop Being Manipulated and Abused - And Start Standing Up for Yourself, "If you live your life to please everyone else, you will continue to feel frustrated and powerless. This is because what others want may not be good for you. You are not being mean when you say no to unreasonable demands or when you express your ideas, feelings, and opinions, even if they differ from those of others."

Sometimes, for me, pleasing others means that I can't be happy if they are unhappy. *I know that living like that is simply insane.* I mean, so many people are unhappy *at any given moment*. How could it possibly be useful for me to join them? What good could come of it? And yet, I've experienced this when I have a disappointed client, an anxious child, or my partner is upset about something at work.

I've been learning that it's very important for me to remain at peace (as best I can), no matter what is going on or what anybody is telling me to do, feel, think, or say. That's my only true power. With my inner peace intact, I can be useful. I can also powerfully bear witness to the truth others are sharing with me. This is my *sankalpa* or intention every single time I do yoga: "I am at peace, no matter what."

Whenever I *lose it*, my youngest, Charlie, always reminds me to, "Breathe, Mom!"

For me, this is the work of a lifetime.

# Co-Dependency can be SNEAKY

I feel like the un-boundaried state of co-dependency needs more exploration because it's soooo sneaky! The desire to fix *or* to the tendency to have pity on somebody who is suffering are just two of the ways we can act co-dependently. Co-dependency is really when we step on the boundaries of others by being in their "business."

Empathy is wonderful, and we want to have empathy. Dr. Marshall Rosenberg, who developed Nonviolent Communication (NVC) says, "Empathy is presence. Pure presence to what is alive in a person at this moment, bringing nothing from the past."

Simply bearing witness to a person (empathy) and not giving advice or adding in any reaction (such as, "That's horrible!") is the ideal way to be empathic. But so few of us practice that sort of listening.

I have been practicing bearing witness with my coaching and teaching groups, and people report that they feel so much safer when others simply listen to them with zero feedback.

We can offer a response like, "I'm sorry you're experiencing this." Or "I can see that you really feel hurt by this." But jumping in to reassure the person or to fix is not nearly as powerful.

## Dear Magnificent Me,

Do you ever feel like **you get co-dependent**? **Who** are you most likely to act that way with? What could you **try the next time** you are with that person?

## Dear Great Mystery,
Please help me to BEAR WITNESS to others' suffering,
and keep me out of the mire of co-dependency.

*No. 187*

# Boundaries As BRIGHT lines.

In the past four years, I've become a huge fan of *bright lines* when working with myself. I was introduced to this fabulous term by Bright Line Eating's creator, Dr. Susan Pierce Thompson. Here's how she explains this concept in an online interview for Women's Health Network:

"I got the idea to create Bright Line Eating when I had just finished reading a book called *Willpower*, by Roy Baumeister. There's a chapter that notes how Eric Clapton said he needed 'bright lines' when it came to his sobriety."

The term "b*right lines* is a legal term used to describe a clear, unambiguous boundary or rule that you apply consistently to produce predictable results. From my own experience living free from food obsession, I knew that having bright lines could help you lose weight and keep it off. Sure, you have to eat to live. But you don't have to eat doughnuts!…. Bright Line Eating talks about creating clear, unambiguous boundaries that you just don't cross. The four Bright Lines are: eliminate sugar, eliminate flour, set up a schedule for your meals, and weigh your food."

**SO, BRIGHT LINE =** A clear, unambiguous boundary or rule that you **APPLY CONSISTENTLY** to produce predictable results.

Maybe you have a bright line with your antiaging facial oil, you always put it on before bed, no exceptions. Or, with your dogs, they get two walks a day, no matter what the weather is. Or with money, you never make an unplanned online purchase without waiting 24 hours.

Bright lines are a lot like having a personal policy and can reduce friction in our lives as we practice them diligently. This practice results in automaticity which takes the boundary load off our frontal cortex and reduces the need for willpower. Brushing your teeth is probably a bright line for you already. Where else would you like one?

# Dear Magnificent Me,

Where do you **wrestle to stay in integrity** with yourself by yielding to your own self-declared bright lines. (For example, do you keep drinking when you promised yourself, you'd drink only one glass of Pinot Grigio?)

What bright line are you interested in **creating**?
Or what established bright line would you like to **honor** yourself for?

# Dear Great Mystery,

Please help me keep MY LINES BRIGHT AND SHINY.
I know I do better work in the world
when I'm integrity with myself.

KNOWS HERSELF!

MANHANDLING CARP WITH EASE.

"WHEN I KNOW WHO I AM, I BECOME NATURALLY BOUNDARIED"

— MOLLY DAVIS

@SARAH SEIDELMANN

### KNOW YOURSELF
#### and your boundaries will come naturally.

Therapist Molly Davis (of @BoundariedBootcamp) say, "When I know who I am at a deep level, I become boundaried—I know where my boundaries are."

I wrote about why knowing ourselves is often hard but important work in my book *Born to FREAK: A Salty Primer for Irrepressible Humans*:

> Something I've learned about those who, like me, were born to FREAK i.e., those of us who were put here on Earth to restore balance to the Earth by expressing our utter uniqueness! is that we often have a poor sense of ourselves. Perhaps it's because we can be porous (not unlike Sponge Bob), merging with the universe until we have trouble seeing who we really are. I've learned that it's very good to know what our own gifts are so we can get down with our DIVINE PORPOISE.

Many things have helped me figure myself out. *Knowing thyself is fucking powerful*—it can clear a lot of confusion out of the way and unlock a lot of doors. It's also a bit of a process. Sometimes messy. (Bring extra napkins.)

There are so many ways to discover what your gifts are, but perhaps none so powerful as simply asking the people who love you. Yes, actually ask other people 1) what they experience when they're with you, and 2) what they think your strengths and gifts are. *Being born to FREAK, we may have previously gotten quite a bit of negative feedback*. We may have a poor sense of ourselves as a separate individual and find it difficult to see who we really are.

# Dear Magnificent Me,

Would you be willing to **ask some people you trust** those two questions listed on the left? You could offer to do it for them in return.

When have you experienced a moment where you thought, **Wow, I am really being myself right now!** I'm bringing my gifts to this world!? When you were in that moment, what sorts of boundaries do you imagine you might be capable of **creating and holding?**

# Dear Great Mystery,

Please show me how to get to know myself in a deeper way. Who am I? Help me to answer this question.

Imagined conversation between an Al-Anon sponsor + sponsee

SARAH SEIDELMANN

We don't have to FORFEIT OUR PEACE FOR ANYONE.

Inspired by Melody Beattie's "Codependent No More"

Phillip's obsession with his guinea pigs is out of control. I must be vigilant.

# mind your OWN BEESWAX

Because my grandmother was an alcoholic, I attended my first Adult Children of Alcoholics (ACOA) in college. I went to my first Al-anon (a twelve-step meeting for people who are worried about another person's drinking) meeting in my forties, and more recently I went regularly for two years. *What a gift!*

The principles of Al-anon taught me so much about boundaries.

For one thing, boundaries are not only external, with others, but can also be *internal*. For example, I can notice when I get triggered by a person, institution, TV show, etc., and ask myself what disturbed me about that.

Usually, my own *big* reaction is a strong clue that I'm out of bounds—I'm in somebody else's business (or God's business, a place I tend to go; *I, or more accurately my ego, wants to control everything!*).

These internal boundaries are most precious. And it takes practice to become aware of them. The surest way to make ourselves bananas is to get involved in other people's business, and the fastest way to become peaceful again is *to tend to our own lives.*

### Dear Magnificent Me,

Who or what has **triggered the heck out of you** lately? Whose business were you in? (The other person's? God's?) Who do you know who skillfully stays out of other people's beeswax? What would it look like to **take a page from their playbook** in this situation?

### Dear Great Mystery,
### when I'm tempted to obsess over somebody else's problems,
### remind me to FOCUS ON MY OWN AFFAIRS.

*No. 195*

# the DALAI LAMA Has Boundaries
## lots of them.

I have spoken to so many people, *including myself*, who believe(d) they are being nice in their choice to be completely (or partially) un-boundaried with another person. Research shows, Brené Brown tells us, that simultaneously having zero boundaries with a person and being kind to that person is basically impossible in the long run. Research also shows *that the kindest humans in the world are actually the most boundaried.*

"What? How can this be?" we all cry and gnash our teeth. "You mean the Dalai Lama has *boundaries*?"

Yes, he probably has a healthy firewall, including thirteen secretaries to keep folks at bay. He's *that* compassionate. Without any boundaries, you're at high risk to become an exploding doormat.* Make a boundary instead. The discomfort you will feel is short-term and the real compassion you'll exude will make you proud of yourself in the long run.

*My beloved mentor, author Martha Beck, calls the special brand of resentment that comes from not having boundaries "exploding doormat syndrome." Once resentment arrives, we're at risk to eat/drink/shop/act out over it *or* have the resentment come out sideways (that's the *explode* part!).

### Dear Magnificent Me,

If you trusted that the **more boundaries** you have, the **more compassionate** you can be, what boundary would you **erect today**?

### Dear Great Mystery,
Please help me to make and uphold healthy boundaries every day so that I may grow in compassion for myself and others.

*No. 197*

# WHY did i do THAT?

Exploring *why* you may have been saying yes when you really mean no is a powerful exercise. Here are a few typical struggle scenarios of yes/no:

***Should I volunteer to chair that committee,*** or is my ego getting more out of this than the cause and I really need downtime instead, since my mom just died and I'm exhausted?

***Can I truly afford to give that client a discount***, or am I caving just to avoid confrontation? Will I feel resentful later?

***Do I want to go part-time***, or am I scared if I take my boss up on the offer that I'll lose respect with the team…. but I also want to be home with my new baby.

***Do I truly want to go to Hot Goat Yoga out at the farm,*** or am I just afraid that if I say no my friend will never call me to ask to do something again?

Whatever the feeling is that has you stuck between yes and no—guilt, obligation, pride, confrontation avoidance, FOMO, etc.—pay attention.

Once you are aware of what is beneath your knee-jerk yes, you can stop saying yes when you mean no.

If your yes or no is still unclear to you, even after hashing it out with a friend, working with a therapist or life coach can help you figure out what's going on.

Together, you'll figure it out and get a strategy for setting a boundary when your

yes is a *really* a no.

# Dear Magnificent Me,

Name a pattern you see in yourself around when you say **yes but you really want to say no.**

What would you like to do **differently**?

# Dear Great Mystery,

Please show me where I am **thwarting myself** and give me the courage to honor my own needs and **preferences**.

# DETACHMENT *preserves* LOVE

There can be no great boundary-setting without a metric ton of detachment.

Detachment plus self-love seem to be key.

These words by Melody Beattie, from her book *Codependent No More*, help:

> "Detachment is a key to recovery from codependency. It strengthens our healthy relationships--the ones that we want to grow and flourish. It benefits our difficult relationships-- the ones that are teaching us to cope. It helps us! ... We learn to let go of people we love, people we like, and those we don't particularly care for. We separate ourselves, and our process, from others and their process. We relinquish our tight hold and our need to control in our relationships. We take responsibility for ourselves; we allow others to do the same. We detach with the understanding that life is unfolding exactly as it needs to, for others and ourselves."

My beloved sponsor Judy often says to me (after I have told her about *the insane thing* that another person did),

"People are going to do what people do, Sarah."

I need to adopt this attitude if I am going to have any sort of peace in my days here on planet Earth.

I can love myself enough to set myself free from hand-wringing and judging others for whatever they are up to.

I have enough trouble on my hands right here with me.

*No. 202*

 # Dear Magnificent Me,

Who do you need to **detach from with love**?

What would that look like and **what would change**? (For example: I'm anxious about my daughter, who's in college and I've been offering her unsolicited advice about her future career. I commit to only listening and not offering advice unless asked.)

 # Dear Great Mystery,

Please help me to LET GO of control. Help me to allow others to be how they are.

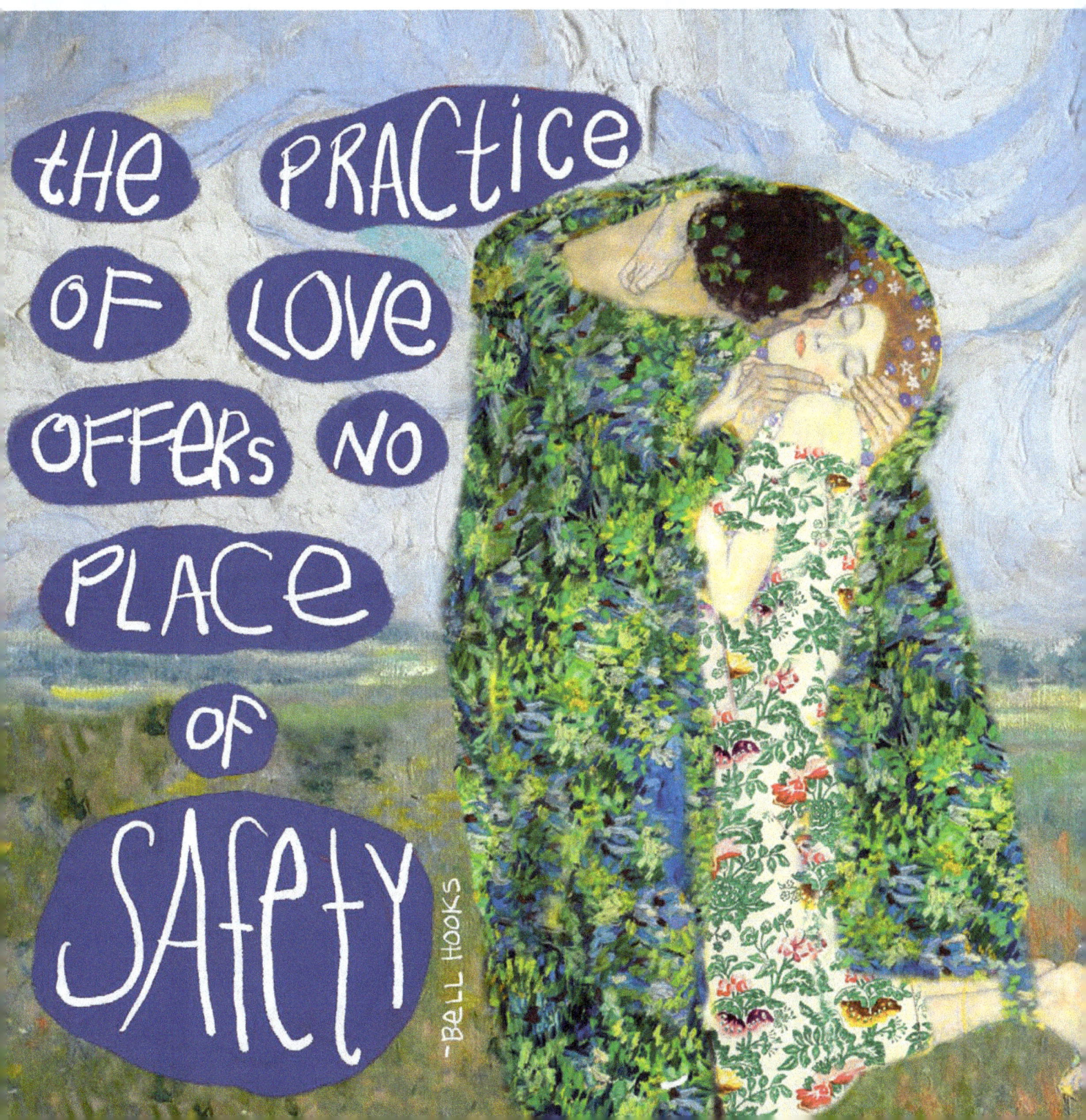

# Safety is **NOT** guaranteed.

This project has transformed my most precious relationship and I am feeling extremely grateful. During this project, my husband Mark and I discovered that we both needed more boundaries. More spaciousness. In this moment, by choice, we are sleeping separate rooms so that we can each have our own quiet time. Oddly, this has brought us closer together. We still spend lots of time together at home and have several daily love rituals that help us stay connected! Our relationship is being reborn after 33 years.

I loved reading bell hooks' book *All About Love*. The thing about love is that it isn't safe. It's vulnerable. And hard. We may put up a boundary and the other person may decide to walk away. Or maybe somebody we deeply care about put up a boundary with us and we are bereft. It is not safe to love, but it's the only legacy I believe I can leave.

### Dear Magnificent Me,

What boundaries have you put up that allowed **more love to flourish**?
(For example, maybe you stopped loaning money to your brother and now you go hiking together instead of fighting about the money he owes you.)
In your loving relationships, where might a boundary move you from **resentment back into connection?**

### Dear Great Mystery,
Please give me the courage to **love freely** and unabashedly.
Help me trust that I am always safe.*

*Please note that this does not apply if you don't feel safe in a particular loving relationship. In that case, reach out for help.

# boundaries make TRUE Intimacy Possible.

A friend shared this exquisite quote with me, by Esther Perel: "When people become fused—when two become one—connection can no longer happen. There is no one to connect with. Thus, separateness is a precondition for connection: this is the essential paradox of intimacy and sex."

This is the basis for what Esther says about intimacy: if we want to have untamed lives in our bedrooms, we'd better stop being so domesticated in the rest of our lives. Let there be mystery and intrigue!

For me, spending time alone and going off on my own adventures (and seeing my husband Mark do the same) makes our relationship more interesting. Then we have things to report and new experiences to share with each other. In our case, If we do everything together in lockstep, we both feel stifled.

### Dear Magnificent Me,

Is there a place in your life with a romantic partner or a dear friend where you could use **more separateness**?

Is there something that **no longer works for you**? What would it look like to **shift** that?

### Dear Great Mystery,
Please give me the courage to honor both my own ALONE-AND-AWAY TIME as well as that of my partner (or child, parent, sister, friend, etc.).

*No. 207*

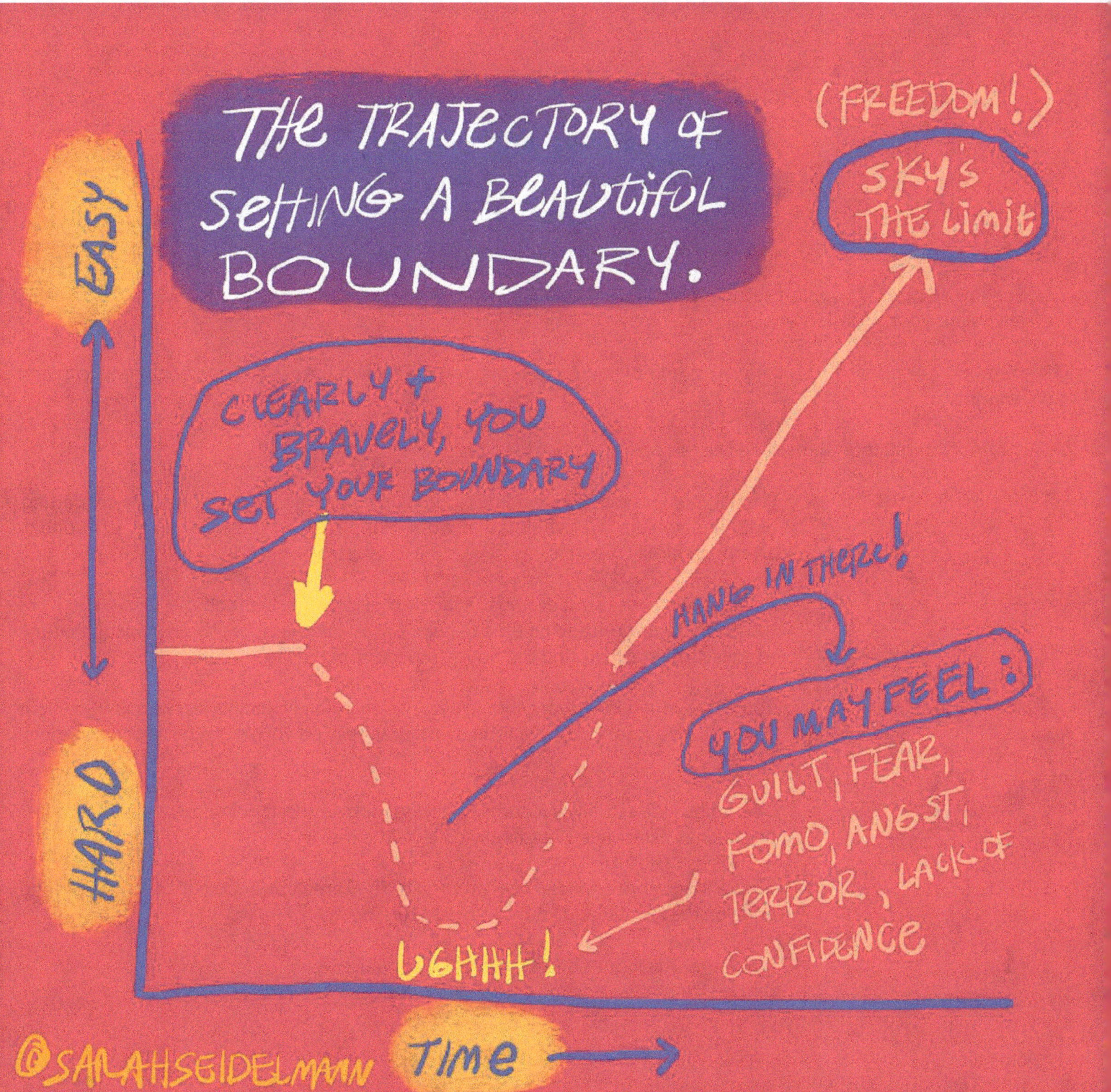

# The Trajectory of Setting a Beautiful Boundary.

- **Y-axis:** Easy ↕ Hard
- **X-axis:** Time →

**Clearly + bravely, you set your boundary**

**UGHHH!**

**Hang in there!**

**You may feel:** guilt, fear, FOMO, angst, terror, lack of confidence

**Sky's the limit** (FREEDOM!)

@SARAHSEIDELMANN
No. 208

# The Discomfort IS temporary.

Life begins on the day you start setting some boundaries. But, as the graph above depicts, there will be a dip (usually) after you put your boundary in place.

Remember: *The discomfort is temporary, and the outcome is awesome*. The outcome is your personal freedom and sovereignty.

This journey might look something like this:

**SETTING YOUR BOUNDARY:** You tell your kids that you're going to be asking more of them because they are getting older and you are overwhelmed at work. Hand out chore assignments at a Sunday afternoon family meeting.

**UGH (PUSHBACK):** An argument breaks out during the family meeting. The kids complain that they have too much homework and no time to help. You assure them that there is adequate time to collect the trash around the house and vacuum the living room.

**GUILT/FEAR/ANGST:** You wring your hands, worrying. Are you being unfair? I mean. your kids are excellent students. You toss and turn a little overnight, worried you might be asking too much of them.

**UPWARD TRAJECTORY:** One of the kids actually vacuums the living room without being reminded. The other one whines extensively, but finally collects the trash.

**FREEDOM:** The kids must be reminded now and again. They aren't perfect, but things are getting done on the regular and your sanity is returning.

**WINNING:** When the oldest goes off to college, he's appalled that his roommate has "no clue how to clean."

*Et voila!* Your job is done!

 # Dear Magnificent Me,

When have you experienced the discomfort of putting up a boundary? What did you feel? (For example, when your teenaged daughter told you were selfish after you set your boundary and you worried she could be right.)

If you didn't cave in after that discomfort, but continued to hold your boundary, what did the outcome of having the new boundary do for you?

Where do you need to be willing to feel uncomfortable and put up a boundary now?

 # Dear Great Mystery,

Please put me on the path of willingness to say no or to ask for what I need and to sit in the discomfort of that **without back peddling**. Thank you!

forward peddling!

"Assume that the other person has no idea what your boundary is."

— Nedra Glover Tawwab

Sarah Seidelmann

# make BOUNDARIES CLEAR

"Gah! Why does he *never* knock on the door before he comes into my office?"

"I wish she would have told me it was going to be a cocktail party. I've only got 22 days of sobriety and I'm feeling shaky. She *knows* I'm an alcoholic!"

"If my kid calls me one more time saying it's an 'emergency' and asking for money when I'm at work, I'm gonna lose it!"

Many of us complain, vent, and whine about people who frustrate us. We *assume* that *they should know better* than to disrespect our boundaries. But frequently, we have never explicitly told them what our boundaries are. We haven't clearly said, "This is what I need…" or "That doesn't work for me because…" or "I don't like it when you…"

**Therapist Nedra Tawwab says that** *we must assume* **that others have** *no clue what our boundary is.*

That's because what's right for you might be utterly wrong for another person.
Boundaries are very personal preferences.

## Dear Magnificent Me,

Have you been **explicit enough** with your work colleagues, teenagers, partner, mother, or friend about your boundaries? Where might you need to **state a boundary more clearly?**

## Dear Great Mystery,

Please give me the courage and tenacity to CLEARLY ASK for what I need from people.

# boundaries can TAKE TIME

When we ask somebody to change their ways, it can take some time for them to get used to the new way.

When we become adults, we often change (becoming more of who we really are!) and it can take our families time to adjust to new boundaries, like a change in our pronoun preferences, for example.

And, of course, some folks may not be interested in honoring our new request and our boundary. If we give them a chance, but they show us that they don't want to change, then we must decide what we will do to take care of ourselves.

Maybe we have a new eating preference ("I'm vegan now" or "I don't eat sugar") or we would like the house to be quiet during our work Zoom calls. Whatever the change your new boundary requires of people, you may have to gently remind them a few times before it becomes a habit for them.

### Dear Magnificent Me,

Can you remember a time when **somebody asked you to change** the way you did things in order to honor their preferences and y**ou had a hard time adjusting**?

**Can you offer patience to others** when you make boundary requests?

### Dear Great Mystery,
### Please give me the personal awareness to honor the boundary requests of others.

*No. 215*

extraverted and introverted
# BOUNDARIES

Boundaries in relationships can and should be lovingly tended. We don't always want exactly the same thing as someone else—that would be so boring!—but we can ask for what we want and need.

In my relationship with my husband Mark, I tend to be the extraverted one, more prone to wanting to throw dinner parties and go out on the weekend.

It's taken a lot of practice to figure out how to honor my own (sometimes) more outward needs in collaboration with Mark's (sometimes) more inward needs.

We do host dinner parties. They require two yeses—one from each of us.

More often, I get my extrovert kicks by going out to lunch or dinner, going out to parties on my own, and attending shows or art gallery openings with friends.

## Dear Magnificent Me,

If you didn't have to consider anybody else's feelings,
**how would you want to spend the upcoming weekend?**

## Dear Great Mystery,
## Please help me get my needs met IN A WAY THAT HONORS ALL OF US.

*No. 217*

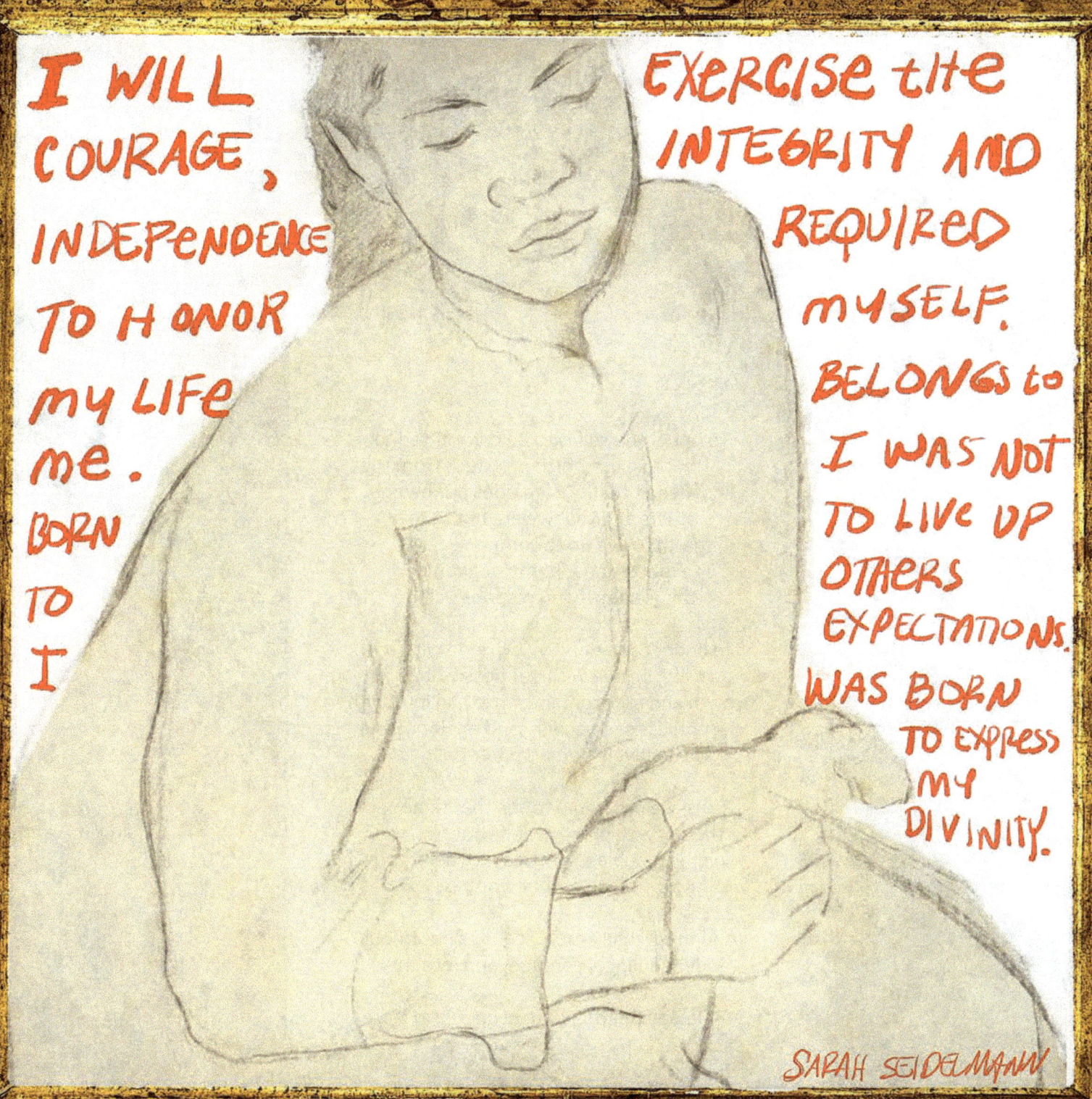

# HONOR THYSELF

To honor the self is to be committed to our right to exist which proceeds from the knowledge that our life does not belong to others and that we are not here on earth to live up to someone else's expectations. To many people, this is a terrifying responsibility.

To honor the self is to be in love with our own life, in love with our possibilities for growth and for experiencing joy, in love with the process of discovery and exploring our distinctively human potentialities.

Thus, we can begin to see that to honor the self is to practice selfishness in the highest, noblest, and least understood sense of that word.

And this, I shall argue, requires enormous independence, courage, and integrity.

—Melody Beattie, *Codependent No More*

# IT'S time to FLY

I have a hunch that if you've been reading this book, you might already be making some better-boundary waves in your own life. Maybe you've been daring to say no more often. Or maybe you've created personal policies/bright lines about certain things. People will probably notice the pep in your step, and when they do, tell them about the shifts you're making.

Let's normalize saying no.

We all need friends like Cousin Harriet who can show us the way.

**If you wanna *fly*, you're gonna need some serious boundaries!**

Have a great boundary story?

If you tell it, please use #boundariesmakelovepossible in your post at Instagram

or Facebook and tag me.

I want to hear it!

@sarahseidelmann at Instagram

## RESOURCES

**Al-Anon.com** – I cannot tell you how grateful I am for this twelve-step recovery group. The meetings are online (or in person), and free, and happen all over the world. If you love somebody who is addicted, or if you simply cannot rest and be happy until another person changes their ways, this program could be hugely helpful to you.

**Boundaried.com / @BoundariedBootCamp on Instagram** – Each day, Molly creates an illustration to help us learn about self-respecting boundaries, and she's even got a bootcamp to help with practicing boundaries in a safe space with other like-minded humans. She offers personal coaching too. I highly recommend her work.

## BOOKS

**Set Boundaries, Find Peace: A Guide to Reclaiming Yourself**, by Nedra Glover Tawwab – From the book: "A little secret from a therapist: Some people would rather end a relationship with you instead of respecting your boundaries. Setting a limit with someone can threaten their ego, and the boundary can seem like an attack on their character instead of a way to preserve the relationship. Healthy boundaries might seem offensive to some relationships. It's not me; it's a rejection of my boundaries."

**Transform Your Boundaries**, by Sarri Gilman – From the book: "We take care of our feelings, our boundaries take care of us." I also recommend Saari's TED talk on boundaries.

**F*ck No!: How to Stop Saying Yes When you Can't, You Shouldn't, or You Just Don't Want To**, by Sarah Knight – What HelloGiggles says about this book: "Say no without being an a**hole and save yourself from burnout with pep talks and sage advice."

**Daily Rituals: How Artists Work**, by Mason Currey – This book showcases the pitfalls of having no boundaries with yourself *and* the glory of having just the right amount of boundaries, by sharing the amazing daily habits of many famous artists +creatives through time. An addictive read.

**The Way of Integrity: Finding the Path to Your True Self**, by Martha Beck – This amazing book can help you become more aware of where you are out of integrity with yourself and where you might need better boundaries. It's an incredible read about finding your way to happiness. If you can be honest with yourself, things are going to get a lot better.

# Thank You YOU
### and thank you.

Dearest Reader,

**I am grateful for you!**

I hope that after reading this little book you feel excited and a lot more courageous about putting up boundaries. The thing I keep learning is that boundaries truly do preserve love in our relationships! Funkily enough, the boundaries we create make love and intimacy *grow* and expand in more ways than we can imagine.

You've got this!

I hope you **talk about** boundaries with your friends, partners, and family members. We can all learn from each other. Together, we get better.

My writing/creating is reader supported. If you enjoyed this book, please consider:

Leaving a book review on Amazon or Goodreads (those help authors so much!)

Gifting this book or recommending it to others

Posting an image of the book and sharing (briefly) why you liked it on social media

You can find me on Instagram at @sarahseidelmann, and at "Sarah Seidelmann" on Facebook.

Please visit me on my website at FollowYourFeelGood.com, where you can find all of my books, a card deck, an app (all about the Beasties—the spirit animals who cross our path to help us), and my artwork.

I invite you to subscribe to my twice-monthly newsletter filled with feel good ideas and resources.

*No. 225*

# SARAH Bamford SEIDELMANN

*Sarah is wearing her own art!*
*"You're not crazy you're co-dependant."*

 Sarah Seidelmann is a true medicine woman and everything she creates is good for what ails us."

Martha Beck, New York Times bestselling author of *The Way of Integrity*.

Sarah Bamford Seidelmann MD is a 4th generation physician, accomplished writer, shamanic healer, artist, and coach. Her six books have all been instant Amazon best-sellers. Her *What the Walrus Knows* app for iOS has users in 65 countries.

For twenty years, Sarah was a board-certified pathologist (what she calls a "disease hunter"). After decades of seeking out illness, she grew curious about *what creates health*. Through her own investigation and with the help of her spiritual ally, Alice, an elephant in spirit form, she discovered that *creative self-expression is fundamental to our vitality and health*.

Sarah specializes in helping others foster a connection to spirit by spending time in nature and observing the birds and animals. Sarah has been an instructor and curriculum creator for Martha Beck's Wayfinder Life Coach Training and an official contributor for Maria Shriver's Architects of Change. She co-leads a creative community called SHINE for writers and artists who are committed to showing up for their work, no matter what.

# Thank You!

Working on this book reminded me of how much I have grown since I completed the "My Summer of No" 100-day project in 2022. I would never have had the chutzpah to write this book were it not for encouraging conversations with so many of you on Facebook and Instagram. You showed me with your messages, comments, and emojis how much the boundary project was helping you change your life as I changed mine. THANK YOU SO MUCH!

I want to give a deep bow to editor **Grace Kerina** who is the kindest and wisest soul. Her methodology is MAGIC for me. She makes book-finishing feel fun!

Thank you to **Deanna "Drai" Ambrosio Schindler** of Wild Redhead Design. She knocked it out of the park and is a Sacred Sister. I am deeply grateful for her work.

Finally, thanks to **Mark** for loving me and having my back in every way possible.

# Sarah Seidelmann Collection

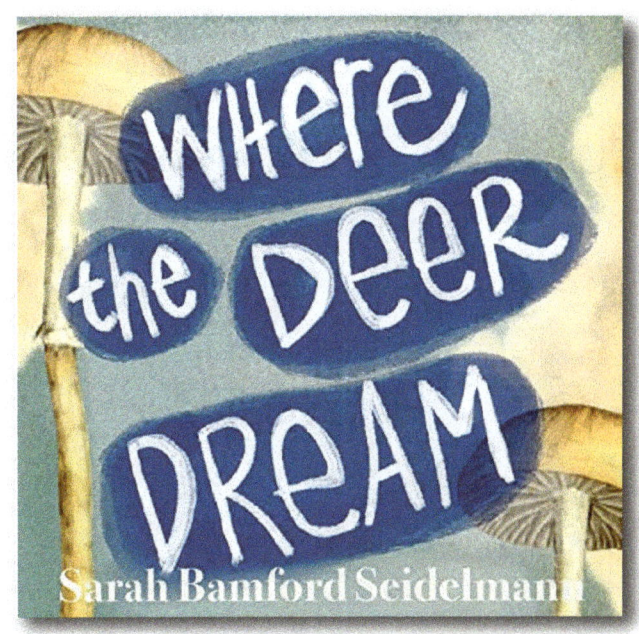
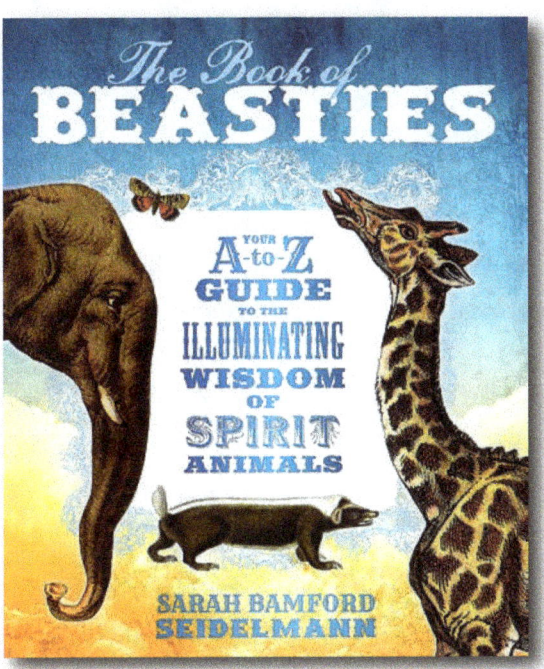

@AMAZON

No. 228

# WHAT THE WALRUS KNOWS
## App for IPAD & IPHONE

Based on Sarah Seidelmann's "The Book of Beasties: Your A-to-Z Guide to the Illuminating Wisdom of Spirit Animals" (Sounds True 2018)

Beasties show up in your life every day—each one carrying a message tailor-made just for you. A message brought by a Beastie may be about beauty or family or work. It might make you smile. It might offer you guidance on a prickly problem. Often, the message is powerful.

Skeptical? That is just perfect! Give it a try and see if the messages help you to find your feel good faster. How do you get messages from Beasties? Do you have to go live out in the woods? Nope. Beasties and their helpful messages will come to you wherever you are. All you need to do is tune in. It can change everything. Curious about how? Open the app and dig in.

Some cool features in the app:

- A cross-referenced Field Guide to Beasties
- Pull a Beastie "Card" to ask for help (Divination function)
- An integrated Journal to keep track of past divinations and your results/insights.
- A 16 minute guided shamanic meditation to help you discover your Core Beastie

*This mystical book/app has the energy that's needed right now.*
*– Mary Ellen Telesha*

$4.99 – iTunes

**4.8** ★★★★★ out of 5

*No. 229*

Printed in the USA
CPSIA information can be obtained
at www.ICGtesting.com
LVHW080018131124
796475LV00042B/1667